The Dating Guidebook

Tips For Living a Happy and Healthy Single Life Without Losing Yourself in the Dating Process

The Dating Advice Girl

authorHOUSE®

AuthorHouse™
1663 Liberty Drive
Bloomington, IN 47403
www.authorhouse.com
Phone: 1-800-839-8640

Published by AuthorHouse 2/21/2013

ISBN: 978-1-4817-1166-1 (sc)
ISBN: 978-1-4817-1168-5 (e)

Library of Congress Control Number: 2013901617

Dedicated to my mother, Dr. Beverly Tillman. Thank you for inspiring, supporting, and believing in me. You are the reason this book made it to print.

Contents

FOREWORD

Singles! Why aren't we having fun out there?! Why do we put so much pressure on ourselves and on our dates? On first dates, the main objective should be to get to know our date…not whether you'll go out on a second date or whether he or she's "The One." When we are busy looking for "The One," we miss the joys and perks of being single. We need to remember that the beginning of a courtship should be more about enjoying ourselves and getting to know our date than foreshadowing what will be. This obsession about what will be in the future, overshadows what actually is in the present moment! Why put unrealistic pressure on ourselves and our dates? The single life can be the most exciting and memorable period in your life if you allow it to happen! The dating possibilities are endless if you allow yourself to be open to them.

You may be asking yourself, "How is The Dating Advice Girl able to enjoy the dating process, when I have such a hard time with it?" First of all, I'm not too selective when it comes to a specific type. I am however, a bit more selective when it comes to my love interest's personality, character, and integrity. I've dated many different ethnicities, nationalities, and personalities who all had very different occupations, looks, mindsets, temperaments, passions, and quirks. I've learned a lot about the dating process by choosing to be open-minded on dates. Besides being more interesting and fun, open-mindedness gives you many more options to choose from.

I'm also able to find the positive in all dating scenarios even the bad dates. I find that it's extremely rare to meet singles who can recognize and appreciate the good that comes from all dating scenarios yet still be realistic. I always get excited about the possibilities when I meet someone new. Every new relationship is a new adventure and I treat it as such. I don't bring an overabundance of baggage to new relationships and I treat the first date as if it was my first date in life. This is the key to enjoying the dating process.

I truly believe that each new relationship should start with a clean slate. I allow myself to be open to the possibilities, which can be risky, but it's a must if you want to connect with someone new. I do fall in love a little with everyone I date, but I wouldn't have it any other way. I've had long-term partners, but I've also had short-term relationships that have been just as meaningful as those that were long-term.

One day you may want to settle down into monogamy and possibly even matrimony. Until then, take your time, be selective but reasonable, and remember to have fun along the way. It's important to be present during this important period of discovery and growth. Embrace your single status and all that comes with it. These can be the best years of your life if you remain open.

Whether you love being single or hate it with a passion, I guarantee that there will be something that you can relate to in this book. We have all been on bad dates. We all need a confidence boost from time to time. We've all experienced a dating slump and we've all been confused as to how someone feels about us. Remaining present and realistic is what allows singles to enjoy the dating process. My goal is to help you to make the most out of your single status without losing yourself in the dating process. My hope is that you will fully embrace your single status, after reading this book. This is your introduction to the dating process.

CHAPTER 1

ARE YOU HAVING FUN YET?

When was the last time you were truly present on a date? What if your focus was simply to get to know a potential new love-interest? What if you challenged yourself to go on a date with someone you never thought you'd like and were pleasantly surprised once you got to know them? Just think how different a date could go if you made lighthearted fun your objective rather than unrealistically trying to 'husband' or 'wife' your date on Date #1. Making the conscious decision to be present, positive and proactive, especially during the early dating process, guarantees that you will have some great times with some amazing people. This can drastically change your love life. The goal should simply be to get to know someone better. Everyone has an interesting story to tell. Learn your date's story. Have a drink or two if you're so inclined, relax, and simply enjoy their company. Having fun on dates is all about your mentality. It's choosing to enjoy each moment along the way even if you don't see yourself ultimately with this person. Cut yourself a break and have some fun!

Rest assured, nobody really knows what they're doing when it comes to dating. Everyone could use a little guidance in the early months of the dating process. Yes, some singles may have more developed interpersonal skills or pick-up tactics than others, but because the dynamics between every couple are different, each relationship is a new experience with new strengths and challenges. Given this fact, most of us learn as we go. We could avoid so much heartache if we would simply remain present, keep an open mind and realize that dating in the early months should be about getting to know someone new. My goal is to help you to rediscover the fun in dating and give you the tools to get the most out of your dating life.

WHY SINGLES HATE DATING IN THE EARLY MONTHS

The first dates with your love-interest should be seen simply as a 'get-to-know-you' session. Dating should be easy and fun! It shouldn't be filled with drama, tears, and overall unhappiness. That is what makes dating a horribly unpleasant process. In the first six months of a relationship, YOU SHOULD BE HAVING FUN AND GETTING TO KNOW YOUR LOVE-INTEREST! If you are willing, you can have fun with almost anyone. Even if you don't plan on going out a second time with your date, why not make the best of the first? You may have absolutely no intention of seeing your date again, but that shouldn't stop you from enjoying a night out on the town.

Dating can be hard, but we make it harder than it should be. In the early dating months it can be difficult to decode dating behaviors especially if you lack the right dating tools. This is the time period when singles tend to form negative opinions about the dating process by getting caught up in 'where things are headed' rather than being present and focusing on getting to know a new love-interest. Dating becomes fun when you have reasonable expectations. Your goal should be to experience something fun and connect with someone new. As the dating process progresses, you will naturally start to discover whether or not you have met a possible match who has similar likes, dislikes, and relationship objectives. When you are able to let go of possible future outcomes, dating becomes light-hearted, exciting and fun!

The majority of singles hate the dating process. Is it because there really aren't any quality single people out there, or is it a lethal combo of pessimism, fear of dating and of rejection, unrealistic expectations, and a lack of dating know-how? It's this combo that makes single people detest their single lives and makes singles want to run away from the dating process. It's time to change your perspective and start enjoying your single years instead of avoiding or dreading them. Let's say you are single from college graduation until your mid-thirties. That's more than a decade of singlehood... how will you spend it? Pissed off and bitter.... or happy with a variety of experiences, a network of great friends and exs, and contentment in knowing that you've enjoyed a single life that your unhappily single friends would kill for. I've chosen to live my single life through the latter example and so can you!

You hold the key to happiness in your dating life. When you've reached a level of contentment within yourself, then and only then can you truly find successful relationships. This book will help you tap into that happiness through the following 6 objectives,

- *by showing what you do and don't have control over when it comes to men, women, and the dating process*

- *by giving you the tools to empower yourself in spite of any dating dramas that may present themselves*

- *by showing how we share the same experiences as single people to create a sense of community*

- *by showing how fun the dating process can be if you're open to accepting fun as an option in your dating life instead of seeing dating as something to be feared or dreaded*

- *by giving examples for you to discover your likes and dislikes, negotiables and non-negotiables in regards to dating and relationships*

Let's get started by reviewing some common dating terms...

DATING DEFINITIONS

What's the difference between 'seeing each other' and 'dating'? What does being single actually mean? How do you know if your relationship qualifies as an exclusive partnership? Someone might be a 'friend with benefits', but if you see that person only on a sporadic basis, do they become a 'one night stand' instead? Effective communication is the most important part of trying to figure out what's happening with you and a love-interest, but part of that communication is to have an understanding of what certain dating terms mean. Here are just a few definitions that may come up while you're navigating the dating scene.

2nd Date Hint/Follow-Up Date Hint-After a first date, rather than actually asking a love-interest out for another date, one of you hints that you'd be interested in going out again. You may mention that you can't wait to see a certain movie or try a new restaurant. The 2nd date hint, or Follow-Up Date, is a subtle way to encourage your love-interest to ask you out rather than you doing the asking.

Blind Date-This is a date that involves going out with someone you've never met face to face prior to the first date. The date has been arranged through friends, colleagues, or even via an online dating or social networking website.

Booty Call-The booty call usually occurs late in the evening, usually after the bars have closed and things are slowing down for the night. Both parties are in agreement that this meeting is only for sexual purposes. The two parties know each other on some level but the interaction is mainly sexual. The purpose of the booty call is to release sexual tension. This may or may not involve sleeping over at each other's places after sexual events have occurred. This is similar to Friends with Benefits, but you might not consider each other friends. It's different from a one-night stand in that it could happen on a regular basis.

Celibacy-This is the conscious choice to abstain from sex for spiritual, religious, or personal reasons. Usually used to gain clarity of thought and mind, celibacy is different from a dating or sexual dry spell because you are consciously choosing to abstain.

Cougar-A cougar is the controversial term referring to a woman, usually over 40, who regularly dates men several years younger. There is usually a large age difference between a cougar and her love-interest...generally 15 years or more.

Date-A date is a planned or scheduled social meeting between two people with the intention of getting to know each other better and possibly getting involved romantically.

Dating- 1. Although there are many definitions for this seemingly simple word, dating is when you spend time regularly with a specific person in romantic scenarios, including but not limited to dinner, movies, and sexual encounters. The dating period usually lasts a few to several months before either progressing to something more serious or dying out. It can go on for years without changing status. To date someone is to have the intention of developing some level of emotional, sexual, intellectual, and/or spiritual intimacy. 2. Another definition of dating is often used to describe one's relationship status. For example, you might use the word 'dating' as a verb and not in regards to anyone specific you are dating. i.e. "I'm newly single and currently dating."

Dating by Default-When you don't date consciously, you date by default. You're essentially 'going along for the ride' rather than actively choosing who you date, what you want to do on your dates, and who you want to be when on dates. Dating becomes unpleasant or even disastrous when we date by default and choose not to have a say in what happens in our dating lives.

Dating Dry Spell-Otherwise known as the dating slump, this is the period of several months to several years when you aren't actively dating. The dating dry spell is less of a choice and more of a default status.

Dating Overlap-The dating overlap occurs when you start dating someone new before your current relationship has officially ended. It's the brief period when you are seeing two people at once while you are transitioning from one relationship to another.

Exclusivity-This is when you and your love-interest make your relationship official, in the dating sense. You agree to date only each other. The two of you are in a committed relationship.

Follow-up Date-Another term for the second date with a new love-interest.

Friend Zone-When a potential love-interest plays it too cool and casual, doesn't drop enough hints, or isn't upfront about his or her feelings, he or she can indirectly end up in a place where the new relationship turns into friendship. The friend zone can be avoided if genuine romantic interest is expressed and a clear romantic gesture is made.

Friends with Benefits (FWB)-This is when you and an established friend, decide to become sexually intimate with each other without defining it as a relationship. The FWB shift usually occurs when both people are in a dating slump or are actively not dating. It can be a way to satisfy a sexual urge with someone you know and trust without having to be in a relationship.

Going Dutch-This is when you and your love-interest pay for your own date-night expenses while on a date together. Usually associated with dinner, you may choose to go dutch for financial reasons or to keep things platonic and on a friend-level. Going dutch sets a tone for the date and is generally used in more casual dating scenarios.

Hibernation-The several month to several year time period where you choose not to date for personal reasons ranging from focusing on personal growth to fear of dating due to bad past relationships.

'On a Break'-You and your partner are not officially broken up, but you are taking time apart to figure things out in terms of your relationship. Though your status is not single, this break is typically used to put your relationship into perspective, to work on problems individually or possibly to see what it would be like to live without your partner.

No Strings Attached (NSA)-This refers to a sexual encounter without a relationship and usually without knowing much about the other person. These interactions are strictly physical with an understanding that all you want, expect, or need from the other person is purely sexual.

Open Relationship-This involves two people who are in a relationship, but they're also able to date other people. These two people openly discuss their boundaries and set the terms of their openness in regards to what lines can and can't be crossed emotionally and sexually with other people. Both verbal and written agreements can be made to make sure terms of the relationship are clear to everyone involved. Outside partners are aware of the couple's relationship status.

Relationship Maturity-This refers to a person's emotional and behavioral maturity in a relationship. Age does not necessarily correlate with emotional and behavioral maturity. It has more to do with the way in which a person handles disappointment or issues in a relationship. Everyone has their own pacing in terms of relationship maturity. A mismatched maturity level could lead to misunderstandings and frustrations.

Single-To be single is to be free in body, mind, and spirit to meet, date, and be sexual with any other single person of your choice without having to 'answer' to anyone. It's not being committed, married, or engaged. You could be dating someone and still technically be single. A person is single until two people agree that they are 'no longer single' and are only dating each other. Until this talk happens, you are technically still single. You can only give up your single status if you choose to give it up willingly.

Social Media Etiquette-This refers to the posting, commenting, and communicating respectfully on friends, colleagues, and love-interests' social media pages. Just like in life, the objective is to be polite and courteous and avoid posting anything that would embarrass, anger or upset the person you're interacting with.

Wingman-The wingman is someone who aids you in the process of meeting and flirting with a prospective a new love-interest. Helpful in social situations, the wingman is a friend or colleague who knows your strengths and will help shine a spotlight on those strengths to help you win over the object of your affection.

CHAPTER 2

CHECK YOURSELF!

CONFIDENCE

What does being confident mean exactly? Confidence is knowing that you are uniquely special inside and out. It's not caring what people think about you. Just think about the last attractive person who caught your eye…he or she most likely displayed some level of confidence, which in turn made them attractive to you. That person may not have even been classically attractive, but you were still drawn to him or her. Why? Because they have confidence! They are sure of themselves and sure about what they have to offer. They know their strengths and this knowledge gives them an ego boost. Look at anyone that is successful or famous. They know their individual strengths and they have their own individual style and look. We identify with them because they have a unique characteristic that we enjoy or admire. They exude confidence and know that they have something special to offer. You are no different! You should be just as confident. Take notes from these individuals. There's no reason you too can't be someone that turns heads when you walk into a room. Confidence is the difference between those who get their pick of available singles and those who don't.

We all have times when we aren't 100% confident. That's normal! But honestly, if you don't like yourself, what makes you think anyone else is going to like you? To gain more confidence, find the things that you do well and become an expert in these areas. When you have moments of self-doubt, these strengths can be called upon to boost your sense of self-worth. Why not try something artistic? Creating art, making music, or working on a project or hobby are also great ways to build confidence. Building confidence is a process, but it's easier when you have produced a tangible product or accomplished something like earning a degree, learning a language, or creating something artistic. Use your strengths, personality, and style to build your confidence level.

When you are strong and confident, people will either be drawn to your confidence or repelled by it. It's as simple as that! Those who are repelled or indifferent to your level of self-belief will weed themselves out and that makes your job much easier. You want to be with someone who appreciates what you have to offer and is not intimidated by your confidence. Why waste your time with singles that aren't truly drawn to you? There are plenty of people who will think you're fabulous! No one is liked by everybody, so if someone ends up not being interested in you, don't take it personally. You're just not suited to be with each other. On to the next one… There will be people that do appreciate your confidence and those are the people you should choose to have in your life. Do not alter yourself! Don't take it personally. This should not be taken as rejection. You are strong and confident and you deserve a strong, confident partner to compliment you. Someone who is truly confident will love your confidence and won't feel threatened by it. They will like that you know who you are and have a strong belief in yourself. They'll think it's totally hot that you know your strengths and actively embrace your uniqueness. Don't settle for someone who is threatened by your confidence. Be selective about who you invite into your life and choose people that vibe well with your confidence level.

RESPECTING YOURSELF AND YOUR LOVE-INTEREST

Respect is a huge part of any relationship, friendship, or partnership. It's part of the trust building process. When you give respect, you are more likely to get it. How would you feel if the tables were turned? How can you expect respect if you don't give it? So often if we don't like someone, we can be rude or even cruel both consciously and unconsciously. Respect is like karma…what goes around comes around. What do you have to lose by treating someone with respect? It just makes all interactions easier and more pleasant. Kindness is contagious.

Everyone deserves respect; even those that you choose not to have in your life. If someone doesn't treat you with respect, you can still choose to be respectful to him or her. Simply make the decision not to interact with that person in the future. You can always respectfully decline a future invitation. What's the point of being a jerk to someone just because you don't like them? We are still human beings and we all deserve respect…not to mention bad news and bad behavior travel fast. Whether you're in a small town or a big city, eventually word will get around that you have a lack of respect for others, which can lead to a bad reputation.

CHECKING YOUR LISTENING SKILLS

Listening is respect and respect is listening. Another crucial element to giving and receiving respect is being able to listen. Listen to your love-interest and try not to monopolize conversations. If you give your crush the opportunity to express themselves openly, they will probably reveal more than you ever expected. Sometimes we just need to give him or her the spotlight by asking questions and listening rather than talking. You might learn that he or she is deeper than you thought, more intelligent, more sensitive, more of a man or woman than you ever imagined. Try not to overpower them in conversations. Part of effective communication is being able to listen. Nothing is more irritating than someone that isn't listening to our needs, wants, desires, and sometimes our rants. Just because they might not have as much to say as we do, doesn't mean that what they're saying is not important or valid. They might be a man or woman of few words, but those words might be profound. Maybe they have tons to say, but just never felt comfortable or had the opportunity to express themselves. We so desperately want to be heard that we sometimes forget about the other person. If you give a potential love-interest the chance, he or she may surprise you!

PLEASE AND THANK YOU

Our mothers taught us this when we were growing up and it still holds true into adulthood. Always say please and thank you! It's a basic thing and it's so easy to do, yet it's amazing how many of us don't actually say it on dates or to our love-interests on a regular basis. We just assume that our date knows that we are appreciative, or we act entitled as if w deserve everything he or she is offering us because we're so fabulous. Being fabulous doesn't mean that you shouldn't show your appreciation for your date's efforts. He or she wants to treat you to a nice evening out on the town, so why not encourage them to do it again. A simple 'Thank You' can do wonders for encouraging your love-interest to engage in more date night flattery.

DATING YOUR EMOTIONAL EQUAL

A relationship should be fun, sexy, respectful and exciting in the early months and this is only possible with someone who has a similar level of emotional maturity. You may see potential in someone, but he or she might not be a good fit for various reasons including conflicting relationship goals, different emotional needs, or bad timing. Don't force it. It's no one's fault. It's hard to come to the realization that you and a new love-interest aren't on the same emotional maturity level. This may be revealed during an argument or serious conversation when you remain calm, cool, and collected and he or she flies into a blind rage. This person's intentions are not necessarily malicious; it's just better to find out earlier rather than later that he or she might not be the right person for you. Having said this, never disrespect someone because they aren't on the same level as you emotionally speaking. Just let them go and find someone who is! Even if your potential love-interest is only in your life for a short amount of time, he or she should still be on the same emotional maturity level. If you choose to date someone who isn't on your level, be prepared for possible disagreements, arguments, or hurt feelings.

TALKING HONESTLY ABOUT WHAT YOU WANT TO A LOVE-INTEREST

The only way you'll get what you want in a relationship is if you communicate openly with your love-interest. Be clear but respectful when talking about your needs and wants, so your love-interest has all the facts before they make a decision. Don't let assumptions take the place of conversations in your relationship. For example, on early dates, weave the fact that you are not looking for a serious relationship into the conversation if you feel that is something your date should know. If you are open to any and all possibilities state that as well. This way no one can say they were mislead. Oftentimes we are afraid that our love-interest will not be open to hearing what we want or need in a relationship, but how else will he or she know what annoys you, or makes you smile? If we are upfront about what we want and our love-interest wants to make the relationship work, they will enthusiastically meet our demands. Don't let fear stop you from asking for what you want and need from a new relationship. If your love-interest is not interested or not capable of making these changes, then that's a good indicator that he or she might not be a good match for you relationship-wise. If you choose not to be upfront and honest about what you want, the truth will come out eventually.

ACCEPTING CHIVALRY AND SHOWING APPRECIATION

FOR THE LADIES: Sometimes when we get accustomed to being taken out, we forget our manners. Yes, you are amazing and yes your love-interest asked you out and thinks you're fabulous, but that doesn't mean that you should take it for granted. Don't forget your manners! Always be polite and accept date night chivalry and romantic gestures with grace.

Just like you could be out with other guys, your love-interest could be out with other ladies. If you enjoy chivalrous acts, encourage your love-interest by saying 'thank you' if he holds the door for you for example. He'll get the message and will likely want to repeat his chivalrous behavior.

If you aren't into certain acts of chivalry, simply let your love-interest know that certain gestures of affection aren't necessary. If you don't want him to open your door for you, just tell him in your nicest tone that you'll get the door yourself. He should not be punished or scolded for practicing old-world chivalry. He's operating under the assumption that women like certain gestures. If he likes you and he realizes that you don't like or need certain things done for you, he'll adapt to make you happy. Just be respectfully clear.

FOR THE GUYS: Don't be insulted if your love-interest wants to pull out her own chair, pay for her own meal, or open her own car door. Some women you date may want to take care of themselves. It's important not to assume this before putting forth effort though. It's always great to show your manners when meeting someone new. If your love-interest is not receptive or even insulted by your chivalrous gestures, make an effort to understand what she likes or doesn't like and adjust accordingly.

Also guys, when dating you may run into a woman who is unappreciative of your chivalrous efforts. This does not mean that you should stop being chivalrous. Rather than preemptively punish all women that come after your unappreciative love-interest, simply seek out women who are appreciative. There will be women who will take notice of your efforts. A woman who does not offer a 'thank you' or show her appreciation for your efforts is not worth your time. Even if you feel your love-interest deserves special treatment, you should do your best to rise above the madness and stay classy. You are not obligated to go on another date with her if there's a lack of respect. If your date is exhibiting offensive and entitled behavior, follow through with the first date, but don't ask for a second.

FOR THE LADIES: BEWARE OF THE INVISIBLE PRICE TAG

There is a difference between your love-interest being chivalrous and him showering you with material things. When a woman is being pursued in the early months of dating, sometimes a gift is offered. Sometimes guys expect sexual favors or even commitment in return for big gifts. Yes, of course, it's great to be offered material things, but sometimes there is an invisible price tag attached. A gift here or there may be okay, but if you're relying on your love-interest for material things, you may want to make sure it's being offered with no expectations attached.

You should never feel guilt or pressure to accept a gift. Gifts should be offered simply because you want to offer something to someone. When it comes to accepting expensive gifts, be careful. These could also be considered a down payment for sex. It's important to know what you could be getting into before you accept that brand new BMW.

CHAPTER 3

SINGLE AND READY TO MINGLE

It can be intimidating to jump back into the dating scene if you've been off the market for months or possibly even years. If you are starting to date again, the most important thing you should remember is that dating, especially in the early months, should be treated as a 'get to know you session'...nothing more. When dating becomes a fun get to know you session, it also becomes less scary. If you are new to dating due to a recent divorce, separation, breakup, or you simply have a renewed interest in dating; the first step to jumping back into the scene is raising your confidence level *(see Chapter 2)*. Doing something for yourself, learning something new, and conquering a new challenge are all ways to raise your confidence level. When you do something for yourself and only for yourself, not to please your parents, friends or anyone else, you will automatically raise your confidence level. For those of you who are newly single, you may be in somewhat of a discovery period. This is great! Discover new things about yourself. Do something you've always wanted to do...take a dance class, learn an instrument, or learn a new language. When we create and learn, we gain self-esteem. Focus on making yourself better and you will attract both friends and potential mates who will be drawn to this new confident, interesting, and upgraded version of yourself.

GETTING OUT OF YOUR COMFORT ZONE

Are you only meeting the same kind of guy or girl? Do you only date athletes, but you'd like to meet more entrepreneurs? If you've had a string of unhappy relationships with a certain 'type' or are just in a dating rut, do something new and try a new type. It could be the best thing you've ever done to switch up your social life. Maybe you only meet a certain type because you hang out at the same places with the same people. It may be time to get out of your comfort zone and join a new club or start a new activity to meet new people. If you usually hang out in sports bars, why not try a wine bar for a change of pace. A small adjustment to your usual social activities can do wonders for your dating life.

BREAKING THE ICE

It can be intimidating to approach someone out of the blue and ask them out on a date. You're fighting past your fear of rejection, the fear of looking stupid, and the fear of freezing up and not having anything to say. But before you totally freak out, remember that practice makes perfect. With practice and the right communication tools, you can get past your nervousness when approaching a potential love-interest. Some nerves are normal when meeting someone new. Practicing small talk will help you get used to the nervousness you'll feel when starting conversations with new people. It can be hard to think of things to say, when someone unexpectedly catches your eye, but shyness can be overcome with practice. Here are some tips for getting more comfortable approaching and asking out a new love-interest...

1. INTERACT WITH PEOPLE EVERYWHERE YOU GO

Even if you don't specifically find someone attractive, just start talking to all kinds of people about everyday things. The objective is to get comfortable starting a conversation. For example, if you're at a coffee shop, ask someone what his or her favorite coffee drink is. If you're at a shopping center, ask someone where the nearest Starbucks is located. You can use this in any situation *(more examples later in this chapter)*. If you are comfortable talking to anyone about anything in any setting, you will be infinitely more comfortable with those you find attractive.

2. MAKE SURE YOU KNOW WHAT IS GOING ON IN THE WORLD

There are so many interesting things happening right now, from politics to your favorite reality show. There are a million topics that can be discussed. It's all about having a lot of different talking points at your fingertips.

3. ALWAYS TAKE A HINT

If the person you're trying to talk to is in a hurry,

ends the conversation with you, or is clearly not interested in chatting with you...let them go and find someone else who may be more willing to have a chat with you. Remember, there will always be people who won't have time or interest in meeting a stranger. Don't take this personally. Just let those people go and focus on the people who are interested in casual conversation.

When you use these skills in the dating world, it will be very important to know when someone wants to engage in a conversation or not. This all takes practice, but if you start with short casual conversations in everyday situations with both men and women, you'll get more comfortable talking to new people, which will make it easier to talk to those you'll be interested in romantically.

CONVERSATION STARTERS

The early dating process is all about conversation and chemistry. Everyday we interact with people that we find attractive, but we might not know exactly how to start the initial conversation. Your instinct may tell you to use that witty pick up line that you saw on your twitter feed, but honestly pick-up lines rarely work. Your best bet is to practice small talk in everyday situations with everyday people. Be yourself and don't worry about someone not liking you. The emphasis should be on breaking the ice and engaging in small talk with a stranger. If the person you approach has a conversation with you, they may have some level of interest in you. When I say 'some level of interest' that could range anywhere between 'just being friendly' to 'thinking you're interesting or attractive'. If someone doesn't respond or answer your question and walks away, you know they aren't interested in engaging in small talk or anything else. You probably won't know their level of interest in these quick interactions, but all of your future relationship and dating scenarios will start with an initial casual conversation. Getting comfortable chatting someone up should be one of your most important goals. Use these icebreakers as practice for approaching new people and starting conversations.

Here are 4 icebreakers to help you start a conversation when you're out and about. They can be used in other scenarios, where appropriate….

- **IN A GROCERY STORE-***Ask a fellow shopper about a food item they are selecting or if he or she has tried a food item in the aisle they're shopping in ex. If they are looking at chips, you ask, "Have you ever tried these salt and vinegar chips before?"*

- **AT A BAR-***Invite your crush to hang out with you and your friends at your table. If he or she is interested, they will come and hang out with your group.*

- **AT A COFFEE SHOP-***Comment or ask about the book your crush is reading. If he or she is writing or working on something (and you are as well), comment about the writing process or ask him or her what they're working on.*

- **AT A MALL-***Ask someone if they know where a certain store or restaurant is located. You may know where it is, but this is a simple way of striking up a conversation.*

- **EVERYWHERE-***Notice an item of clothing that your neighbor is wearing and compliment him or her on it. Choose something you actually like though. It will seem*

> *disingenuous if you compliment something that you couldn't care less about.*

If someone doesn't show interest in you, don't take it personally. They're simply making room for the right people to find you. You'll never meet those people if you don't make the effort to break the ice or to allow people to break your ice.

ASKING SOMEONE OUT

Yes, asking someone out can be scary, but the more scared you appear to be, the more hesitant he or she will be to accept your offer. When approaching someone new, act as if you're talking to a friend or colleague. Be friendly and confident. No one wants to be asked out by a grouch, a 'Debbie Downer' or someone who expects rejection. The trick is to make sure that your love-interest feels that they aren't being pressured and that they have some level of control over the situation. This will make them feel more comfortable! After a lively ice-breaking conversation, here are 3 things you can do when you suspect someone is interested in you.

1. THE INFO EXCHANGE

Politely ask your love-interest for his or her business card, phone number, or email. In return, offer your business card, phone number, or email. Respect that they might not want to give you certain contact info since you've just met in a public place and possibly in a random way. If he or she gives you their email, send a maximum of two emails following up or asking them out. If you gave your info to your love-interest and he or she contacted you, congrats! Try asking them out using strategy #2 or #3 below. If you don't hear from your love-interest, it's safe to say that he or she is not interested for one reason or another. Don't dwell, move on. This may have nothing to do with you personally…your levels of interest simply don't match up. Continue on your search to find those singles who think you are amazing… you will find them!

2. THE COFFEE MEETING

Tell your love-interest that you'll be at your favorite coffee shop on a certain day or time if they'd like to meet you. Make it seem like you'll be there working on your laptop all afternoon and if they're in the neighborhood and want to say 'hi' that's where you'll be. There's absolutely no pressure involved with this invitation…just a friendly no pressure coffee invite. Just make sure you will actually be at your coffee shop on the day and time you mentioned in case he or she decides to meet you. Nothing's worse than accidentally standing someone up because of bad planning.

3. THE GROUP OUTING

Invite your love-interest to meet you and your friends for a drink. Tell him or her that you and some friends will be at a specific bar on Saturday at 9pm if they want to come by for a drink. Tell them that they are welcome to bring friends.

Telling your love-interest to bring friends will take tons of pressure off of the situation. It's a cool way to see them in action with their friends, see how they relate to others, and to see what their friends are like. Plus, it becomes less of a date and more of a friendly, spirited get-together between friends.

THE WINGMAN

The wingman is an irreplaceable aid to the single guy or gal in finding a date. The wingman is a male or female friend who knows you well, and who will help you meet, get to know, or make a connection with a potential love-interest. Typically useful at parties, bars, and clubs, the wingman can use their wingman powers to help you in any setting ranging from bars to coffee shops.

Your wingman should help you with your goal of winning over your love-interest. He or she should help you in your efforts and should be of support to you in your quest to get to know someone better. For example, if you and your friend are at a bar for happy hour and someone catches your eye, you and your wingman could walk over to say hi. If your wingman introduces you, it's like an automatic seal of approval. Even though your love-interest doesn't know you or your wingman, it still sends a message that you have a teammate that is willing to vouch for you. Your wingman is giving you both a social endorsement and recommendation. Don't let your wingman do all the work. After an introduction, you should take control of the meet and greet scenario. Your wingman should chime in here and there, but be careful not to allow anyone to steal your spotlight.

Your friends can be excellent 'wingmen', as long as they aren't interested in you themselves and things are kept platonic. Guys, a girl friend can be a great wingman! This could put your female love-interest at ease and make her more interested. A word of caution, make sure the interaction between you and your opposite sex friend is platonic. It can be confusing for your love-interest if he or she detects flirtation or jealousy on the part of your wingman. If your wingman acts like more than a friend, the interaction with your potential love-interest will switch from 'interested' to 'not interested' because 'that guy or gal is obviously taken'.

Be aware that your wingman can very easily turn into a 'cock-blocker' if you're not careful. Anyone that wants to help you should have your best interests at heart. Make sure that your wingman doesn't secretly have plans to make a move on your potential love-interest. That's a huge no no! Choose your wingman wisely!

RESPECTFULLY DECLINING A DATE NIGHT INVITE

It's one thing to turn someone down for a date for logistical reasons, but what do you do if you are completely and totally not interested in a suitor on any level? This can be hard if you don't want to look like the bad guy by rejecting someone right off the bat, but let's be real…There are going to be times when you aren't going to be interested in certain singles who ask you out. Don't accept a date based on obligation. It's your job to be discerning and pick those individuals that you are genuinely interested in. Being able to say 'no' to a date is important so that you don't end up doing things and dating people that don't make you happy. These powerful 'No's' will in turn lead you to the people who will make you want to say 'Yes' powerfully. For those times when you're not interested, here are some tips for respectfully declining an invitation for a date without totally devastating your suitor...

REJECTION EXCUSE #1-YOU HAVE A BUSY SCHEDULE

This excuse is the most realistic and relatable because everybody has a million different work, social, and family obligations to attend to. Tell your suitor that you don't have the time to devote to dating right now because your schedule is jam packed for the foreseeable future. If you're never available, your suitor will eventually get the idea.

REJECTION EXCUSE #2-YOU'RE TAKEN

This one is used often because when most people learn that someone is taken, they consider that person 'off limits.' Only use this one if you've mastered the art of the 'poker face'. If your suitor sees through your fib, it can make your rejection that much more awkward for the both of you. If you do decide to use the 'I have a boyfriend/girlfriend excuse,' just make sure to do it convincingly.

REJECTION EXCUSE #3-YOU'RE NOT OPEN TO DATING RIGHT NOW

Saying that you're flattered, but not interested in dating, sends a clear message. You could say that you aren't interested in a relationship at the moment because you're going through a bad breakup or maybe because you're in a 'YOU' phase. Regardless of the reason you give for not wanting to date, your suitor is probably not going to want to navigate through the possible emotional tidal wave that you're implying that you are working your way through. Even though the absolute truth may be that "You're not in a place where you're open to dating HIM OR HER right now," the statement is still true without making the rejection personal.

REJECTION EXCUSE #4-YOU'RE NOT INTERESTED IN YOUR SUITOR

This is the direct and personal version of Rejection Excuse #3 and should only be used if you are 100% not interested in your suitor and you are annoyed or offended by his or her approach. Especially if your suitor keeps pushing you to go out with him or her, this should stop him or her in their tracks. Sometimes the direct approach is the only thing that gets through to someone who is overly aggressive and persistent. There's no need for you to list the many reasons why you're not interested, but if you are direct and honest, your suitor will be more likely to back off.

THE FAKE PHONE NUMBER AND IGNORING CALLS

FOR THE LADIES: It's always better to just say that you aren't interested rather than keep someone waiting by the phone in anticipation. Be respectful! Don't waste anyone's time. Don't give out your number out of pity because your suitor will feel just as rejected if you give them your number then avoid their calls. What is the point? Giving a fake phone number gives your suitor false hope and it just plain makes you look bad. Giving out your number and ignoring your suitor's calls isn't any better.

FOR THE GUYS: There are a few reasons a girl may give you a fake phone number, but it basically boils down to her not being interested. Generally speaking, women do this because they don't want to turn you down to your face. They give their number to avoid any in-person awkwardness. Yes, it's totally misleading and disrespectful for someone to give you their number and then never answer your calls. It would definitely be more straight-forward for them to just say they aren't interested rather than lead you to believe that they will answer your calls and maybe even date you. Don't take it personally. You wouldn't want to date someone who has such bad manners anyway. Don't waste time thinking about someone who is clearly disinterested and disrespectful. Women who are interested will make sure you can reach them easily, will return your phone calls, and will make sure to give you their actual number.

CHAPTER 4

DATING.COM

There's no 'right way' to meet other singles nowadays. Whether you meet someone at your local coffee shop, or virtually through an online dating website, the possibilities are endless. Just like anything, there are positives and negatives attached to all dating methods. Let's look at online dating, the friend or colleague fix up, speed dating, and matchmaking services and discuss how they work.

ONLINE DATING

COST: Free to sign up; fees range from free to $150 per month to correspond with your matches

HOW IT WORKS: This dating method gives you the opportunity to find dates in the privacy of your own home via the Internet. Singles search online through profiles and photos of eligible bachelors and bachelorettes through a chosen dating website. Upload a recent photo of yourself, share basic info and answer questions that will help you to find other singles that have similar interests, beliefs, and lifestyles. Some websites also offer an instant messaging option for those who want to chat in real time with their online crush.

THE UPSIDE: In this day and age of everyone being so busy, online dating is a convenient option. Online dating allows you to speed up the 'get to know you' process as you select and weed out those you find incompatible in order to focus on those that may potentially be a great match. It's also a great way to meet new people outside of your established social circles. Some singles search for sex, some for true love, and others for casual companionship, so you can literally find anyone and everyone online. Luckily there are online dating websites that require singles to go through a rigorous process to find their best possible matches.

THE DOWNSIDE: You can only learn so much about someone virtually. Face-to-face meetings are the best way to really get to know someone. One can only hope that online candidates will be truthful about the information presented in their profile. If you eventually meet them, then it will be clear as to whether he or she looks like the photo or if it's a pic from their college days in 1985. Online singles also have to be cautious about future dates' intentions. It can be a challenge to find singles that are seeking the same sort of interaction that you are looking for.

Here are a few popular online dating websites:

- *www.EHarmony.com*

- *www.Jdate.com*

- *www.Lavalife.com*

- *www.Match.com*

- *www.OkCupid.com*

- *www.SinglesWarhouse.co.uk*

MAKING CONTACT ONLINE

Online messages on dating sites are one way to start a conversation with potential love-interests. A virtual first impression is still impactful and should be taken seriously if you see a person and a profile that seem promising. Your messages are your introduction and that is everything when meeting new people online.

1. DON'T SEND TOO MANY MESSAGES

If you happen to see a few interesting profiles, sending a message is the next step. It's easy to be impatient when waiting for a reply. When meeting new people online, send no more than 2 initial messages...if you don't hear a response, move on to someone else. With online dating as with regular dating, don't wear out your welcome. If you don't get a timely response after two initial messages, assume he or she isn't interested. Find someone else who would be happy to get to know you better.

2. RESPOND IN A TIMELY MATTER

If you are interested in someone, don't let too much time pass before responding to a message.

The more time goes by, the higher the chance your crush might lose interest. He or she may think you are playing games or aren't really interested. It's considered polite to reply anywhere from the same day to a couple of days after receiving the initial message. Remember, you are on an online dating site to meet and get to know new people, not to ignore messages or put people off.

3. AVOID ASKING QUESTIONS THAT ARE TOO PERSONAL

Stay away from questions that could cause a negative reaction, like details of a divorce or your baby mama drama. Check out your online crush's profile and find a lighthearted subject that peaks your interest. He or she is sure to mention something that you'll find intriguing…something that you will both be comfortable talking about. Resist the urge to share every personal detail of your life via online mail. Save a few topics so you'll have interesting things to discuss on your date. There's nothing worse than running out of things to talk about because you were overly anxious during the online process.

4. ONLY GIVE PERSONAL CONTACT INFORMATION WHEN READY

The great thing about online dating websites is that you can correspond on the site as long as you want without giving out your private contact information. Only offer up a personal email or phone number when you feel comfortable, which for some singles may be after the first successful face-to-face date. Others may want to share numbers after a few online messages have been exchanged. Since you are meeting new people virtually, the most important thing to remember is to be smart and safe.

5. SUGGEST A PHONE CALL OR DATE

It can be easy to fall into the trap of only sending messages back and forth and accidentally becoming a pen pal rather than a potential love-interest. At some point either you or your online crush should suggest calling each other or meeting in person. Either one is acceptable whenever you feel comfortable depending upon the conversations and level of interest you have with your online partner. Just a reminder…if someone is genuinely interested in dating you, he or she will arrange to hear your voice and see your face sooner rather than later.

THE FRIEND OR COLLEAGUE FIX-UP

COST: Free

HOW IT WORKS: This is when a trusted friend or colleague sets you up with someone they know. They offer to set the two of you up on a date, because they believe you'd be a good match. You and your blind date have possibly never met or spoken to each other at length. Your first date will be your first time officially meeting each other.

THE UPSIDE: If you haven't been on a date in awhile, what have you got to lose? You never know unless you try. If you trust your friend or colleague you could end up very happy at the end of your date. It's an opportunity to meet someone new and go out for a night on the town. Just be ready for anything and be sure to have reasonable expectations.

THE DOWNSIDE: The Blind Date can be risky and can quickly become the worst-case scenario if your friend or colleague is clueless about your likes and dislikes. Make sure you trust the person fixing you up and know that they have your best interests at heart. Be clear about your likes, dislikes, and non-negotiables. Your date could be everything you feared and more, leaving you thinking, "Wow, my friend must really hate me." Even if you think your friend or colleague is 'well-qualified' to choose a suitable love-interest for you based on your friendship, sometimes their aim can end up way off target. The friend fix-up can work. I have heard of a few success stories, but in general, no one knows who you'll like as well as you do.

SPEED DATING

COST: Small fee for the event

HOW IT WORKS: Various companies organize speed dating events. They usually take place at local bars or restaurants. To keep the interaction to a few minutes or less, the speed dating organizer keeps you on schedule by ringing a bell or blowing a whistle to let you know when it's time to move on to the next suitor. Be sure to keep track of those singles you'd like to see again and those who you aren't interested in. At the end of the night if your match picks you and you pick them, you will be given each other's info, so you can get better acquainted with each other.

THE UPSIDE: Speed dating can be a quick way to meet other singles. You are guaranteed to meet several single people in one night in a fun atmosphere. If you interact with someone you aren't interested in, there is no pressure and no direct rejection because as soon as you're directed to switch partners, you simply circle yes or no on a sheet of paper next to each person's name.

THE DOWNSIDE: Depending on the event and the selection of singles, speed-dating events can be a bit of a downer. You can meet great people, but because it's a 'singles only event,' it can add subconscious pressure to the situation causing singles to seem nervous or desperate.

MATCHMAKERS

COST: Expensive, ranging from several hundred to several thousand dollars depending on the service

HOW IT WORKS: A matchmaker is the most expensive, extensive, and serious option as far as dating is concerned. Because a significant financial investment is required, most participants are looking for a long term or permanent relationship. A matchmaker's success rate is typically over 50% and some boast upwards of 80% in terms of finding a mate for their clients. If you have deep pockets and an eagerness to find a specific kind of partner, you may want to go with this dating option.

THE UPSIDE: This is a great option for singles looking for a serious relationship. Matchmakers do all of the legwork.

They don't have tons of clients at once, so they can really focus on your specific needs and desires. This service can be great for singles looking for something specific and permanent and are willing to pay for it.

THE DOWNSIDE: It can take months to find someone via a matchmaker. Because most clients have very specific relationship requirements, it may take longer to find someone who fits your criteria. The service can also be very expensive depending upon the matchmaker you select.

CHAPTER 5

WHERE TO GO? WHAT TO DO?

The possibilities are endless as far as the 1st date is concerned. Singles tend to go the easy route and do something traditional rather than thinking out of the box. Adding an activity to your date can be a great idea. Doing something experiential where you can learn and create something together helps to build a connection with your love-interest. It's a good idea to take your date's likes and dislikes into consideration when planning a date night experience. Here are some ideas to get you out of your first date rut.

TRADITIONAL DATES

The Dancing Date-There's no better way to connect than with physical touch. Dancing, or learning a new style of dance, is a great way to connect with your date, as long as your date's into it (and has a good sense of rhythm or the willingness to try).

The Bar-Hopping Date-Check out your favorite bars or try out some new bars. It's cool to enjoy a few adult beverages, just do it responsibly. There's nothing less attractive than a date who gets totally out of control and lets drinking take over the getting-to-know-you process. Have fun at the bars, but stay classy.

The Dinner and a Movie Date-This classic date includes dinner, drinks, and a movie. When in doubt, go with what you know.

The Artsy Date-From sculptures and photography exhibits to dinosaurs and ancient artifacts, this date involves something cultural like going to an art gallery, museum, or poetry reading. This is a great way to get to know your love-interest while broadening your perspective.

The Comedy Show Date-Laughter brings people together so this date can lessen the pressure and give both of you a reason to smile and a great way to see if your date has a good sense of humor. It may be wise to avoid sitting in the front row if you don't want a comedian to use you and your date as material in their stand-up act. That could get uncomfortable.

The Happy Hour Date-This date takes place in the early evening hours, possibly right after work, which can be a great way to decompress. Happy hour can be a great first date option because it's early in the evening, which can be less pressure than a nighttime date.

The Night-On-The-Town Date-This date could involve barhopping, stargazing at the viewpoint in your city, or hanging at an all-night diner. You and your date take your city by storm and if you're in a 'city that never sleeps,' you might experience all that your city has to offer into the wee hours.

INEXPENSIVE DATES

The Cooking Date-Skip the restaurant... try a new recipe together. Cooking together is a great way to get to know each other better, plus using hot spices making velvety sauces, and tasting new creations can turn into a very sensual experience. This is a great way to see if the two of you will be a spicy match both inside and outside of the kitchen.

The Picnic Date-For you outdoorsy, romantics out there... buy some wine and cheese, grab a blanket and go to your favorite park. Get to know your date without any distractions and surrounded by nature.

The Home(Work) Date-Feeling unproductive? Why not accomplish something with your love-interest! We sometimes become more productive when working with other people. If you're both entrepreneurs, form your own mastermind brainstorming team. Just make sure you don't completely ignore each other. Check in with one another and make your work date fun and interactive.

The Book Swap Date-Discuss and share your favorite books. Lend one of your faves to your date and see what he or she thinks. You'll get a good idea about who they are based on their opinions, ideas, and feelings in regards to the themes in the book.

The Non-Profit Date-Do something for someone. Make a difference in your community by volunteering together at a homeless shelter, building houses for the homeless, or participating in a community cleanup. You'll know your date is a catch if he or she is excited about volunteering and they think it's the perfect date idea.

The Marathon TV Series Date-Have you fallen behind on your favorite TV series? Why not catch up by watching past seasons with your date? Share the drama of the small screen. This date obviously involves going to one of your houses, so make sure that you are ready to spend a night in.

The Spiritual Date-Share something spiritual together. Maybe there's a special service you think your date would enjoy or maybe you want to gently introduce your date to your spiritual world. If your date is open to it, it can be a very enlightening and bonding experience. It's very important to make sure they would be interested in participating in a spiritual experience with you. A 'surprise' spiritual date could be unsettling if your date has differing views or was expecting a traditional date.

The Coffee Date-Exactly what it sounds like…you, your date, and a cup of java. There's no better way to get to know someone casually than at your favorite coffee shop.

'PLAY' DATES

The Amusement Park Date-Amusement parks can be great fun…eating funnel cakes, winning stuffed animals, riding roller coasters… Just make sure your partner likes roller coasters and doesn't have a weak stomach or a fear of heights, which could make this date nightmarish very quickly. As long as your love-interest knows what they're getting into, this can be a winning date night option.

The Bowling Date-Rent some shoes, pick your favorite ball and get bowling. Bowling can be great fun, again… if your date is into it. This is a great downscale date where you can enjoy healthy competition 'Big Lebowski' style. Later in the night, some bowling alleys have DJs and disco lighting. Let the party begin!

The Concert/Music Festival Date-Why not see a local band together? Be sure to choose a band or event that you are sure your date would enjoy. Seeing a band that your date hates could set a terrible tone for the evening. Outdoor concerts are a safe choice. A jazz spot can be nice too. If the concert is super loud, go to a quiet bar or diner afterwards to get to know your love-interest better.

The Zoo Date-Get in touch with your wild side. Visit the animals at your local zoo and learn something in the process. Before making the trek to your local zoo, make sure your date likes animals, and can cope with funky zoo smells!

UNCONVENTIONAL DATES

The Matinee Date-Daytime dates can be more laid back and less pressurized than nighttime dates. If you have a few hours during the day, why not see a matinee with your date? It's cheaper and you'll probably have the theater to yourselves. Now that's romantic!

The Planetarium/Observatory Date-Stargaze, catch a meteor shower, and learn about the planets on this scientific date. Who ever thought astronomy could be so romantic?!

The Exotic Cuisine Date- This isn't your typical dinner date. Try something new like Ethiopian cuisine or Korean BBQ.

Part of the fun with these cuisines is the preparation of the food or the manner in which you eat it (for example eating with your hands or grilling at your table). Regardless of the restaurant, go light on the garlic in case there's a kiss at the end of the night.

The Casino Date-Only indulge in this date if you and your date can keep the gambling under control. It's a fun venue to get to know someone and share the thrill of 'letting it ride' in a stimulating environment.

The Extended Date-This is a date that keeps going and going in the best way possible. It's the type of date where coffee turns into dinner and dinner turns into drinks. One where you don't notice time passing by. Time flies when you're having fun, and you know you're having fun when you've hit hour 12!

The Booty Call Date-This is the "date" that usually doesn't begin until after midnight and where the objective is sex. It's typically initiated by the 'drunk dial or 'drunk text' and both parties are clear about the purpose of this late night meet-up.

The Wildest Dream Date-This is where your date tells you to dress up, picks you up at your place, takes you to a 5-star restaurant, then to a symphony/opera, Tahiti... whatever. This is your dream date (insert corresponding dream here). Enjoy the fantasy!

The Impromptu Date-The date that is set up at the last minute due to a change of plans, your love-interest just happens to be in your neighborhood, or a long phone conversation turns into, "Do you want to grab a bite to eat?" Go with the flow and enjoy the spontaneity on this date.

The Blind Date-This could be a set up or the first date with someone online. This basically involves any date where the date is your first face-to-face interaction. Truthfully, there is a 50/50 chance of success on this one since this will be the first time you'll be laying eyes on your date.

The Double Date-This date usually involves you, your date, a friend and their date. It can be great because your friend could act as an awesome 'wingman' highlighting your strengths. This date can take some pressure off since there will be three other people on the date. Double dates are great in situations where you've been fixed up on a blind date. It's common to double date with the person that set you up and their date.

The Sporting Event Date-The NBA Finals, The World Cup, The Super Bowl... these are all great opportunities to share in the excitement of competition between teams or countries. There's no better atmosphere for fun than a festive sports' bar during 'the big game.' Not to mention there will probably also be an opportunity to shoot pool, throw darts, or play shuffleboard. Don't forget quarters for the jukebox after the game is over. Go team!

The 'Be A Tourist In Your City' Date- This is the date where you rediscover your city by doing all the things that a tourist would do, but that you've never done. In LA, visit The Hollywood Sign. In NYC, go to the Statue of Liberty. In Chicago, go to the top of the Sears Tower. Head to the local places you'd usually avoid and fall in love with your city and possibly even your date.

OUTDOORSY DATES

The Bicycle (Built for Two) Date-You know the drill. Explore your local landscape as a wheeled twosome. Make sure you're both up for peddling or you could end up exhausted and pissed off that your date literally made you do all the legwork.

The Beach Date-If you live near the coast, why not plan a day at the beach? Watch the crashing waves, catch some sun, or take in a sunset with your love-interest. These dates are about relaxing, enjoying the scenery, and getting to know each other, in a super romantic setting.

The Hiking Date-Connect with nature and get some exercise in the process. Use this opportunity to check out that newly discovered hiking trail you've been wanting to try. Be sure to bring some water and don't start the hike too late at night. Having to be rescued on your date would set a bad tone. Have fun, but stay safe!

The Surfing Date-This one can be tricky. Maybe your date is going to teach you to surf or maybe you're planning on taking lessons together. Either way, make sure you're both excited about swimming, water, and potentially looking stupid or awkward. If you're both on board, get on the board. Surfs up!

The Sports/Adrenaline Date-Do something active like playing football, basketball, or tennis. If you and your love-interest are feeling extra adventurous, go rock climbing, parasailing, or even skydiving. This date includes anything active where you are engaging in friendly competition or participating in a thrill-seeking activity. A little friendly competition and a rush of adrenaline could take your date to exciting new heights!

SPECIAL OCCASION DATES

The Holiday Date (Christmas, Halloween, New Years, Valentine's Day)-There could be a great deal of pressure attached to a first date on a holiday, but it can also be really festive, exciting and full of surprises. It is risky, but it can also potentially be a very fun and festive get-to-know-you session.

The Birthday Date-A bit unconventional... yes! Fun and out of the ordinary... absolutely! If you're sick of typical birthdays and don't have plans, this could be a fun way to start a relationship. Be sure not to make a big deal out of this to your date. He or she could be turned off and confused by the fact that you chose to spend your birthday with him or her so early in the relationship. Bring it up later in your relationship, but until then, it can be our little secret!

The Office Party Date-Spice up a work party by bringing a date. It's super important to bring someone you're proud of that will make you look better since you'll be introducing him or her to everyone. Just make sure to remain professional because your colleagues will be watching.

The Wedding Date-This could either be another wedding guest that you meet at a wedding or a new flame that you invite to escort you to the wedding. Choose a date that will enjoy doing 'the chicken dance' and 'the electric slide' and the two of you will surely become the life of the party.

Don't be afraid to throw out some suggestions for your date. Give your date a few places you are considering and then let him or her choose which one. Especially if you're both a bit indecisive, providing options narrows down the overwhelming number of date night choices and will help you agree on the perfect date night activity.

A WORD OF CAUTION REGARDING BAR DATES

NOTE: *Keep in mind that any date that involves drinks could change the feel of the date. Don't overdo it! Alcohol can lower inhibitions, which can get rid of nerves, but in excess can lead to regrettable behavior. First impressions are very important! Drinking too much on a first date can lead to misunderstandings, moving faster than you'd like sexually, or simply making an overall bad impression. Realistically, there might be times when you or your date might have 'one too many'. In these instances, make sure to have cab fare to get home safely without you or your date getting behind the wheel of a car. Also, consider telling a friend or two where you are going in case of emergency. It's always wise to be prepared so that you're not left in a vulnerable position or a potentially dangerous situation.*

CHAPTER 6

FIRST DATE FUNDAMENTALS

First impressions are everything when it comes to your first date with a new love-interest. Though the first date should be treated as nothing more than a fun get-to-know-you session, you should also do everything you can to make sure it goes smoothly. To make sure you are in a position to have a great first date, here are some general things to remember when on early dates including pre-date prep tips and do's and don'ts while on your date.

PRE-DATE PREP TIPS

Can you believe it?! Your first date with a new love-interest is right around the corner! You're super excited about spending some quality time getting to know each other better, but you're also a little nervous, you want to make sure everything goes smoothly and you want to make sure you're properly prepared. Here are a few last minute tips to help you as your big date approaches...

1. CONFIRM THE DATE

Nothing would be worse than your love-interest forgetting about your date or canceling at the very last minute. Call, text, or email your date to make sure they are still planning for your night out on the town. Don't assume that it's happening. To avoid confusion, confirm to make sure you are still a part of each other's social plans.

2. AGREE TO MEET IN A COMFORTABLE ENVIRONMENT FOR YOUR DATE

Agree to meet somewhere that makes you both feel comfortable. If your date wants you to come to their place, but you'd prefer meeting in a public place, suggest a venue that you'd both enjoy and meet there. Any reasonable person will understand your request. Never agree to a dating scenario that makes you uncomfortable.

3. DO YOUR RESEARCH

Check out your love-interest's social media page, do a Google search or if your friends introduced the two of you, ask them if there is anything you should know about your crush before the date. Any of these things can give you potentially important information about your crush. It can also give you ideas of things to talk about. Facebook can be used to see what your date is up to socially, but be careful! There's a fine line between checking out someone's social media page for conversation starters vs. using it to stalk your love-interest.

If friends set you up, ask them details about your potential love-interest. Perhaps they have information that can help you, like his or her love of Disney characters or their collection of Impressionist art. These things can make for interesting conversations...use that information on your date!

4. DO SOMETHING THAT GIVES YOU CONFIDENCE BEFORE THE DATE

Experiencing pre-date jitters? Do something for yourself to lessen any nervous energy. Go to the gym for a pre-date workout, get a massage to calm your nerves, get a new outfit to present your best self. Especially if you're a bit anxious, treating yourself to something special will boost your confidence before a date.

5. MAKE SURE YOU'RE PREPARED FOR ANYTHING

Anything can happen when you're out on the town with a new love-interest. To ensure things go smoothly, prepare for any scenario including the following...

- *Have specific things with you in case the unexpected happens on your date (that could mean anything from having breath mints, tampons, or 'emergency' condoms.)*

- *Clean your apartment just in case your date ends up at your place later on. You want your date to feel comfortable. Messiness is not a turn on.*

- *Have a few different date night activities in mind in case the first one is booked or unavailable. A backup plan is key. Don't waste time during your date deciding what to do on the date.*

- *Tell a friend your date night plans and who you're going out with for safety purposes, just in case a problem arises.*

HOW TO HAVE A GREAT FIRST DATE

So you've scored a date with a new love-interest and you've picked a date night activity...now it's time for the first date. How do you know it's a date and not just a hang out session? A date is an intentional scheduled meeting between two people with the objective of getting to know each other better on a romantic level. An absence of romantic interest signifies friendship or 'hanging out.' A date can involve dinner, drinks, coffee, an activity, or anything else. As long as there is the intention of moving towards romance, a relationship, or a partnership, anything can be or become a date (*see Ch. 5-Where To Go? What To Do? for more first date ideas*).

Now that the definition is clear, let's discuss the first date. The first date can cause a lot of anxiety, but there's also a lot of anticipation and excitement. Having a great first date boils down to common courtesy, focused attention, lighthearted fun, chemistry, and some level of banter and/or flirting. Of course, you're going to be a bit anxious, but you can minimize the awkward factor and make a good first impression by sticking to a few guidelines on a first date.

1. BRING CASH!

What if you end up somewhere on your date that doesn't accept credit cards? What if you and your love-interest park in a structure or garage that only takes cash? Always have cash on hand, not just a credit card, in case you end up at a cash only venue. What if you and your date carpool and something uncomfortable happens? You want to make sure that you have cash in case you need to get to a more comfortable situation quickly and safely.

2. BE ON TIME

There is nothing worse than waiting for someone who is running late on a date, so do everything you can to be on time. Yes, unforeseen circumstances can happen, but do your best not to keep your date waiting too long. Besides being rude and making your date feel like he or she is an afterthought, it can also put your date in a bad mood and ruin your night out before it even begins. If you know ahead of time that you will be late, call or text your date to give them a heads-up. It's common courtesy.

3. HAVE A GOOD ATTITUDE

So many singles set themselves up to fail on a date, by simply having a negative attitude about what might happen on their impending date. Instead of hypothesizing about what might go wrong on your date based on your 'bad luck' or past dating horror stories, focus on bringing your best self to the date. Hopefully you chose to go out with your date because you had a genuine level of interest and you wanted to get to know each other, right? So based on that, you should feel some level of excitement about spending time with your date. Why even agree to the date, if you're not going to try to have fun?! Don't focus on a hypothetical negative scenario…Seek out and create the joyful moments while on your date.

4. LOOK GOOD AND COMPLIMENT YOUR LOVE INTEREST'S APPEARANCE

Take time to put yourself together for your date. Even if the date is casual and laid back it's important to put together a nice outfit, be freshly showered and well groomed, with hair styled (coiffed bed head is acceptable). If you just stroll in for your date without making an effort, it sends a message that the date is not that important to you. If you appreciate the effort your date has made, compliment him or her on their appearance.

On the other end of the spectrum, you don't want your outside appearance to distract your date from getting to know the real you. Make and effort to look nice for the occasion, but don't go overboard.

5. HAVE FUN

It's dating, not brain surgery! Have fun with it! Dating, especially in the early months, should be a series of fun, get-to-know-you sessions. The moment we start taking things too seriously, too early on, all of the fun goes away. When fun is the goal for your date, the dating process becomes an enjoyable experience and not an unfulfilling, hopeless means to an end. Save the serious stuff for another time and a later date.

6. INTRODUCE EVERYONE

If the two of you are meeting friends at some point during the date, be sure to introduce your friends and DON'T ABANDON YOUR DATE. Even though your friends are awesome and friendly, your love-interest is not necessarily going to have the same comfort level with your friends that you do, so be sure to include him or her in all conversations. Remember, you are on a date. You can hang out with your friends anytime.

7. ASK QUESTIONS AND BE INFORMED

Make sure to ask your love-interest questions about themselves. Don't turn your date into 'The YOU Show'. You'll look like an egomaniac if the conversation is only about you. Also make sure you have some interesting topics to discuss by keeping up to speed on what's going on in the world and in your community. Besides making a good impression, it will also give you things to talk about if the conversation gets stale.

8. LISTEN TO YOUR DATE

Besides being polite, you'll gain useful information if you actively listen to your date. If he or she is telling you that they aren't looking for a serious relationship for example, believe them! They are telling you what they want, now it's up to you to hear them and decide whether or not you're okay dating him or her in the short term or if you'd rather, find someone who shares your relationship goals and objectives.

9. PAY ATTENTION TO BODY LANGUAGE

This one is huge! Try to avoid folded arms, yawning, a furrowed brow, and any other gestures that indicate boredom or disgust. You may be having a swell time, but not being aware of your body language could send the wrong subconscious message to your date. You could be giving potential mates the wrong impression about you. Take a moment to be conscious about your outward behavior and internal feelings about your love-interest. If you are enjoying your date's company, use subtle signs of interest like touching your date's arm, shoulder or back during a heartfelt story. Laughing at your date's jokes, and maintaining consistent eye contact with your date are also positive non-verbal signs of interest. These are all signs that show your date that you are enjoying his or her company. The more aware you are about the non-verbal signals you are sending to your crush, the better you will be able to convey true signs of interest on your date.

10. PAYING THE BILL

Everyone has an opinion about who should pay on a date. I do feel that in guy/girl relationships the guy should pay on early dates, and especially when it's the first date. Another reasonable assumption is that the person who asked for the date should pay for the date. Choosing to pay for your portion of the date for personal reasons, is also a valid choice. Though he or she shouldn't feel obligated, it is also a nice gesture if the person who was asked out offers to make some sort of contribution to the date. Paying the tip on the dinner bill or tipping the valet are both small but meaningful ways to make a monetary contribution on the date. Just remember that the decision you make about paying on the first date will set an important tone. *(see more on Paying On A Date later in this chapter)*

11. SAYING GOODNIGHT AND THE 'FOLLOW UP DATE HINT'

At the end of the date, be sure to make it clear if you'd be interested in another date. If you aren't comfortable initiating the "I want to go out again" conversation, giving your date a 'Follow-Up Date Hint' can give him or her a clue that you are up for another night out on the town. The Follow-Up Date Hint can be something as simple as "I'd like to try that new restaurant you were talking about. Maybe we could try it sometime?" (Feel free to insert any other topic or place that may have come up in conversation during the date.) If your date is also interested, he or she will most likely get the hint and will suggest a specific day or week for a follow up date. Make sure your date has your contact information, so solid plans can be made. A handshake, hug, or a kiss are all acceptable depending on your interest level.

If your date doesn't suggest a follow up date, or if you are not interested in a follow-up date, end the date politely and graciously. There's no reason to burn bridges. If there was some tension during the date and things ended awkwardly, or you were offended by something, just let it go. There's no the point of causing an argument or conflict and wasting each others' time and energy when you can quite simply choose not to go out with your date again. Politely say goodnight and move on with life and move on to other love-interests.

FOR THE LADIES: Your date should pick you up or meet you at your destination. You should not be picking him up or meeting him at his place on the 1st few dates. He should be courting you, not vice versa. It doesn't matter what the excuse is, if he wants to date you, he'll find a way that doesn't involve you driving all over town trying to find him or pick him up.

REMEMBER: Be courteous! You are a team for the night. Don't go on an extended smoke break or get into a long conversation at the bar with someone else. This date should be about getting to know each other better. If you aren't into your date, don't leave them hanging. If necessary, end the date early rather than ignoring or neglecting your love-interest.

WHO SHOULD PAY ON A DATE?

Traditionally the guy pays for the date. Nowadays these lines are blurred. Theoretically the person who does the asking out should pay for the date, but assuming that you both have a romantic interest in each other, it's always best if the guy pays on the first date. If the female pays, the balance of power shifts and it sends a confusing message to your love-interest. Friends split the bill; so paying on the first date could indirectly cause the two of you to end up in the 'friend zone'. If you and your date have more modern ideas about the whole paying thing, the guy should pay for the bulk of the date (anything meal-related or activity-related)…. valet contribution, tip, or movie refreshments is fine for the ladies. Even if it's a daytime coffee date, the same rules apply. Anything else sets up a friendship scenario rather than a romantic scenario.

One reason this 'Who Pays' debate has gotten so heated is because generally the gesture of taking care of the bill is taken for granted. When appreciation is shown, it encourages the person taking you out to want to take you out again. If a gesture is taken for granted, your suitor is less likely to treat you again, and that's when it becomes "every (wo)man for himself." Something as simple as a thank you means a lot to someone who took the time to plan and pay for your fabulous night out on the town.

FOR THE GUYS: While I do understand the economics of always paying for your dates and how that can add up mathematically…chivalry, courtship and good manners trump the numbers on this one. Here are some reasons why you should always pay on early dates, unless you've discussed sharing the costs beforehand…

1. IF EVEN FOR SELFISH REASONS, DON'T RUIN IT FOR YOURSELF

You want to put your best foot forward when dating someone new, right? You obviously don't want to set a bad tone. Regardless of your goal, it only helps you if you are treating your love-interest to an evening of fun. By taking care of the costs associated with the date, you avoid the chance of the dinner bill being the reason for the date going badly. Especially if you seek a second date with your love-interest, you want to do everything in your power to make sure that you are presenting your best self to get to that second, third, and fourth date. If you can consider paying for the date as an inevitable part of the dating process, it may be an easier pill to swallow. You're establishing the role you're going to play if a relationship develops between you and your love-interest. It confirms your role as a gentleman.

2. MAKE SURE YOUR INTENTIONS ARE CLEAR

You're guaranteed to confuse your love-interest if you suggest splitting the bill on the first date. It sends mixed messages. Unless you've agreed to share the cost of the date beforehand, prepare to pay for both you and your love-interest. Some singles assume that if they are paying for their half of the bill, it's a more casual, friendly hangout session than a romantic date. If you are really interested in someone, avoid confusion and take care of the bill. It sends a clear message that you are interested. If it turns out that you aren't as interested as you thought you'd be, follow through with the date, pay the bill, then decline a Follow-Up date.

3. RESPECT YOUR LOVE-INTEREST'S FINANCIAL SITUATION

Especially during tough economic times, it's totally understandable if you or your date want to be more frugal. However, I feel strongly that the person inviting someone out should be prepared to cover the cost of your night out especially if they are choosing the venue, restaurant, or event. When inviting someone to be your guest, you are agreeing to treat them to an evening out. If you are not intending to pay for the date and you are asking someone out, it's only fair to be clear up front. Keep in mind that your date may not be financially prepared or able to cover the cost of the date you've planned, but beyond that, it's a little rude to blindside your date. Any additional contribution your date may make is an added bonus. It's okay to accept any financial contributions if your love-interest insists on contributing, but otherwise only plan a date that you are comfortable paying for in its entirety.

It's polite to pay for the first date. To be clear....we aren't talking friendly hang sessions or even hookups...we're talking about official ask outs to dinner or any other one-on-one social meeting where romance is part of the deal and where you are trying to become a part of your love-interest's life. Yeah, she's a modern woman, but do you really want things to be weird starting at Date #1? Be a gentleman on the first date. If she doesn't appreciate it, then simply don't ask her to go on Date #2. It's that simple. It leaves a bad taste in a girl's mouth if her date doesn't make the first financial contribution. Whether your goal is a relationship or short-term fun, paying for the first date only helps you in the end. You want to set yourself up for success and if that means treating your date, so be it. But wait…what do you do if a girl asks you out? She asked you out so she should pay, right? It's my philosophy that even if your date asks you out, if you agree to the date, you should plan to pay for the bulk of the date. If she doesn't like the idea of you paying, then agree to let her pay for at least a portion of the date. Don't let ego get in the way of making a connection. Paying on a date is simply a part of the dating process.

FOR THE LADIES: There's nothing more unattractive than someone that feels entitled and doesn't express gratitude. Your love-interest wants to spoil you…they just want to know you appreciate it. Why not tell your date that you respect his or her gesture?! If the tables were turned, you would be pissed if your love-interest didn't at least offer a "Thank You" after you treated them to a fantastic meal. Right?

Regardless of how you feel about paying on a date, it's all about manners! In dating, as in life…always put your best foot forward, then adjust accordingly if your efforts are unappreciated. It's harder to make up for a mistake after the fact than to simply prevent it from happening from the start.

THINGS TO AVOID ON THE FIRST DATE

Ah the first date! If you want to make a good impression there are a few topics that should be treated delicately or avoided altogether because they are almost always guaranteed to change the mood of the date for the worse. Talking about an upcoming court date or a big blowout fight with an ex will not help you make a good impression. Yikes! Keep early conversations light and airy. To avoid awkward situations like these, here are a few things you may want to avoid discussing on a first date:

1. AVOID THE EX TALK

Don't talk about exs, other dates, or other hot guys or girls on your date. There's no better way to make your date feel uncomfortable. Even if your date is open-minded and doesn't mind talking about your celebrity crush, it's better to keep the focus on him or her rather than comparing and contrasting with an A-List celebrity, or even worse an ex.

2. CELL PHONE ETIQUETTE

We all have cell phones and we are all busy, having said that, being on your phone constantly during a date is a huge no-no. Unless you are a surgeon who is on call the night of your date, there is no reason you should be answering your phone in the middle of a date. If you do get an important call, politely excuse yourself and handle your business away from your love-interest. Text messaging also can wait. No one appreciates back-to-back phone calls, texting, and checking your phone for messages when you are supposed to be connecting with the person across the table from you.

3. UNWANTED DIET TIPS

Unless your date asks for workout or nutrition tips, don't go on an hour monologue about your workout routine, vegan diet, or make any references to sugar as being 'evil'. The minute you start lecturing your date about these subjects, you are in great risk of accidentally offending your date. It's awesome that you feel great about your six-day-a-week weight-lifting schedule and the fact that you only drink diet soda, but your love-interest will probably feel a bit awkward if you're talking about this just as he or she orders a slice of red velvet cake. Your date can see that you take care of yourself...there's no need to brag or lecture.

4. AVOIDING 'FOOT IN MOUTH'

Think before you speak. If you have even a small inkling that something could offend your date... don't say it!! You have the power to stop 'foot in mouth' syndrome just by taking a moment and considering your date's feelings before you speak. If it could be offensive, avoid saying it.

5. SHARING TMI (TOO MUCH INFORMATION)

Don't share overly personal information about yourself on early dates. Certain subjects can end things before they start. TMI (too much information) can be the death of any potential in a new relationship. These topics include:

- **YOUR TICKING BIOLOGICAL CLOCK**

It's important to have personal goals when it comes to dating and relationships, but don't let your desire for marriage and kids take over your date. A premature commitment talk will put off your date and possibly curb any interest he or she initially had for you. Your date may want to get married and have kids one day, but no one wants to feel pressure from someone they've just met on Day 1. If you've been married before and have kids, it's okay to bring them up in conversation, just don't let others become the focus of your date.

- **YOUR MEDICAL HISTORY**

Talking incessantly about medical issues can be a huge buzz kill. No one needs to know about your restless leg syndrome or your bout with gout. Besides sounding like a sickly complainer, sharing info about your various ailments will not make you appear more attractive. Keep the conversation positive and avoid any cringe-worthy subjects that will most certainly turn off your love-interest.

- **POLITICS AND RELIGION**

If you and your love-interest can discuss these two subjects respectfully, they aren't totally off-limits. The problem is that these subjects sometimes get people so fired up that the discussion gets personal, which can instantly suck the fun out of a potentially great evening. Take care when discussing such sensitive topics. It can be the difference between an informed, stimulating conversation and a bitter argumentative hate fest.

Steer clear of anything that would make your date uncomfortable or something that would cause anything other than a good time. No tales of tragedy or highlights of a recent arrest. There should be a reasonable feeling of safety on your date, not feelings of fear, danger, or disgust. Remember your goal is to have fun and get to know each other…not to frighten, gross out, or shock your date. You only get one chance to make a first impression, so make sure it's a good one.

SLEEPING WITH SOMEONE ON THE FIRST DATE

NOTE: *This section is not intended to advocate casual sex. Since sex and intimacy are an important part of dating for many singles, it is important to discuss the realities of what can happen when you meet someone you connect with.*

When it comes to sex and intimacy, it's important to choose your partner wisely. It's not that difficult to find someone who is *willing*. The hard part is finding someone that is *worthy*. Choose a partner who has some level of class. For example, certain conversational behaviors translate to bad bedroom behavior. Hogging the conversation can translate, to being a hog in other situations. Not listening in a conversation can translate to not listening to your needs while intimate. Even in NSA scenarios, find out everything you can about your partner. Get together in a non-sexual capacity at least once before getting it on, so you can see if any blatant red flags are present. A face-to-face meeting will very quickly determine whether or not you are attracted to someone's energy, if you feel comfortable with your partner and if you are both interested in taking things to another level. It's true that, you won't know all the ins and outs of your partner, but you will be better able to make a reasonable assessment. *Always remember to use protection.* As long as you act responsibly and respect yourself and your partner, things should go smoothly. This is your own personal business and as long as you are safe, you are free to enjoy whomever you choose.

If you and your new love-interest get sexual before you both are ready, you run the risk of that defining your relationship, so be cautious about 'first date hookups' with love-interests that you might want a relationship with. Only a small percentage of relationships begin after a first date hookup. Yes, it does happen, but don't do it because you think it's going to make things permanent. It may accelerate your situation, but possibly only in a sexual way. Only choose to engage in casual sex if you can handle any outcome that comes your way and don't attach any unrealistic expectations to the encounter. *(See Chapter 8-Sealing The Deal for more on sex on early dates)*

BEING STOOD UP

We're all heard horror stories where singles have been ditched on a date. Maybe you were ditched. Maybe you did the ditching. Maybe you've wanted to, but your conscience just wouldn't let you stand someone up. During the dating process, it's inevitable that we are going to go on a date with someone that we just aren't clicking with. Whether it's a blind date, an online date, or someone we thought we'd connect with, there will sometimes be a moment where you want to abort your dating mission and flee as soon as humanly possible. Before you actually do ditch your date, remember that he or she has feelings too. They made space in their schedule to hang with you. You made a commitment to meet and spend time with them, so follow through with the date…then you're free to live your life after that the date is complete.

If you've been stood up, consider yourself lucky that you found out early on who your love-interest really is in terms of their integrity. He or she has done you a big favor. Yes, it sucks to be 'rejected', but it would suck even worse to waste your time with someone who isn't interested, has bad manners, and doesn't follow through with a commitment. Move on to someone who is interested.

CHAPTER 7

FOLLOWING UP FAVORABLY

You've prepped for your first date, you've gone out on your first date, and now you are in what some consider the hardest part of the first date process...the post-date period. It can be the most nerve-racking time because you aren't totally sure how your date felt about you, you're wondering whether or not you'll go out on a second date with your love-interest, and you're trying to be cool and not overanalyze every little thing that was done and said during the date. It's agony to hypothesize endlessly about what that weird inflection in their voice meant or why he or she waited 5 days to call you. We've all be there. This over-analysis can drive us insane.

If you are interested in a second date with your love-interest, you want to play it cool, but not so cool that you confuse your love-interest. Here are a few things to remember while you're navigating through the post-date period.

1. THANK YOUR LOVE-INTEREST FOR THE DATE

After your date is complete, it's nice to call or text your date to say how much fun you had. Your new love-interest will appreciate your kind words. It will also show him or her that you really enjoyed the date and that you are possibly interested in going out again. A word of caution though…one appreciative text or call is enough (see #2). This one call or text will help to see if the two of you are on the same page and want to continue seeing each other.

2. DON'T CALL OR TEXT INCESSENTLY

It's very easy for a simple follow-up phone call to multiply and become a barrage of unwanted calls and texts. Don't overdo it. Your love-interest got your message. If for some reason your love-interest doesn't return your call or text right away, don't freak out. You don't know what is happening in his or her world. If you're too aggressive with the phone calls and texts then you run the risk of either annoying or scaring off your new flame. Make one good phone call, leave a voicemail, or send a text saying that 'you had a great time and you'd love to do it again' and leave it at that. If your love-interest is interested, he or she will respond favorably in a timely manner.

3. PLANNING A FOLLOW-UP DATE

Let's assume you've gotten great feedback from your follow-up phone call or text. During that conversation you and your love-interest agree that you'd like to go out again. Don't wait! Suggest or agree to a date within a week of your last date. Yes, you both may be busy, but the more time that goes by between the first date and the Follow-Up Date, the more opportunity you're giving your love-interest to meet someone else who is more interested, more available, and more eager to make plans for another date. Even if you only have time for a coffee date, or happy hour drinks after work, it still sends a message that you would like to continue to keep seeing each other and that you're willing to fit your love-interest into your busy schedule.

4. KEEP LIVING LIFE

Just because you've met someone you are interested in doesn't mean that life, as you know it, should end. Keep hanging out with friends, keep pursuing hobbies, and if you feel like you need a distraction, go out on a date with someone else. Continuing to date can actually help you decide how much you like your original love-interest. All of these things will help to keep your world as normal as possible while you wade through this period of excitement and uncertainty with your love-interest. When you keep things 'normal,' you can more easily decide how much time and space you are willing to make in your life for your new love-interest.

5. ACTIONS SPEAK LOUDER

If you're not really sure if your love interest likes you, pay attention to his or her actions. After your first date, you should be in touch with each other within a few days and you should have an idea of when a follow up date may happen. If a week or more goes by before your love-interest contacts you, you are not on his or her priority list. C'mon…there are endless ways to communicate with someone. Everybody has a phone, email, social networking page and so on. With all of these communication options, the only way that you should accept not hearing back from a love-interest for more than a week is if they are in a remote jungle somewhere where there is no phone reception. Seriously though, our actions teach people how to treat us. Don't remain available to someone who doesn't treat you with respect or just disappears after a date.

It doesn't mean your love-interest hates you if they don't call you (or return your call right away). It just means that there are just other things, and possibly other people in his or her life that are more important at that moment in time. This is the brutal truth. It's up to you to realize this and accept it for what it is in the present moment…possibly a potential friendship, or a relationship of convenience. If that's not okay with you, move on to the next available candidate. If you are okay with these categories, take it for what it is and don't get pissed off if they aren't 100% available emotionally or physically. Actions speak louder than words and these actions are making it clear that you hold a specific ranking compared to other things and people in his or her life. He or she might be fond of you, but fondness does not equal romantic interest.

If your love-interest doesn't seem interested in going out again, don't dwell on it. Consider your date as practice for upcoming dates with others who are more suited to you. Not every pairing will be the perfect match. But for those who are right for you, a classy post date follow-up can make all the difference.

TEXTING VS. CALLING

We all have busy schedules, but you should make an effort to pick up the phone and have a conversation with your love-interest. A phone call is always the best way to contact someone especially if you're interested in dating him or her, especially if you're calling to ask someone out on a date. It adds a personal touch and shows a level of interest that simply can't be matched through a text, email, or instant message. Yes, those other forms of communication are convenient, but also pretty impersonal. Things can get lost in translation if you are having text-only conversations. Texting has its place, but voice-to-voice contact is the way to go. If your love-interest isn't calling you on a regular basis, it may be a sign that they are only interested in a casual relationship. Having said that, here are a few scenarios where texting instead of calling can be okay...

- *You just want to say a quick hello or follow-up after a date*

- *You're over your cell minutes and you can only text*

- *You're in a loud environment and you won't be able to hear a phone conversation*

- *You forgot to say something or want to ask a quick question*

- *You're making plans to see your love-interest or you want to tell him or her that you're running late or have just arrived*

- *You're at work and it is inappropriate to make phone calls*

FOR THE GUYS: It takes courage to call a girl and ask her out on a date or call to follow up with her after a date, but that's simply an occupational hazard when it comes to dating. It's about taking chances. Yes, the girl could reject you, but you have to take a risk to get the reward. A girl does not want to date a guy who is too afraid to approach her, call her, and ask her out. Part of dating is for a man to show what he's made of and 'fight' for a woman's affections. It's your job to win over her affections and set yourself apart from the crowd. One way you can do this is to call your girl and ask her on a proper date. You'd be surprised at how many guys immediately take themselves 'out of the running' by making the mistake of only texting her. Ladies pay attention to these things. These are the things that keep a girl interested and make her want to get to know you, date you, and be intimate with you. Remember your actions have a direct effect upon what will happen between the two of you.

DATING IN THE AGE OF SOCIAL NETWORKING

Let's assume that you've secured a Follow-Up date and you and your love-interest have plans to go out again. This is a tricky time period where you're excitement can take a turn and a huge online shift can occur. Maybe you've become social media friends so you now have 24-hour access to see what your love-interest is doing socially when you're not together. A lack of social media etiquette causes so many issues with new couples. Especially if you are seeing someone new, it can be hard to deal with the random things that are posted on your love-interest's social media page. So much could be avoided if certain photos and comments were never posted, but unfortunately the two of you may have different ideas about what is appropriate social media etiquette. Here are some tips to improve your online etiquette when dating someone new...

- *Keep your private life private! If there is anything you'd feel uncomfortable with a love-interest seeing, don't post it on your social media page!*

- *Focus more on interacting in person than online with your love-interest. Don't let a potential relationship become a virtual relationship. Put away the laptop and do something together...in person!*

- *Be respectful of the content you post on your love-interest's social media page. He or she may have family members who may see whatever you are posting. Avoid embarrassing him or her and yourself indirectly, and use discretion when posting content on a love-interest's page. It may come back to haunt you!*

- *Don't become a social media stalker! Make a conscious decision to limit your time on your love-interest's page. This can be difficult, but too much time on his or her page can make you crazy creating stories about who's posting things on their page, who's flirting with them, etc. Don't make yourself crazy creating unnecessary drama.*

Once things progress with a love-interest, it may be a good idea to have a conversation in regards to your online and social media activities. If you are seeing someone who is using certain sites haphazardly and it's bothering you, it may be smart to subtly bring it up in conversation. Maybe you're uncomfortable with your love-interest still keeping an active online dating profile and you'd like to discuss possibly closing your accounts. It's sometimes easier to bring up difficult subjects if they are brought up in a fun and humorous way. Saying something like, "Wow! I saw some of your social media photos and it looks like you're having fun without me," can bring light to a potentially heavy conversation. Again, only say something like that if you can say it with a lighthearted tone. A serious tone could make you seem jealous and needy.

Above all, try not to let social networking overshadow actual face-to-face interactions. Dating is about connecting with another person, emotionally and physically while sharing ideas, feelings and experiences. Only so much of that can be done online. Real connections can only happen in-person.

CHAPTER 8

SEALING THE DEAL

GETTING OVER POTENTIAL AWKWARDNESS

Things get less awkward the more you get to know someone. Having said that, early sexual experiences usually have some level of awkwardness simply because you are still getting to know each other, you're finding out each other's likes and dislikes, and you're revealing (literally and figuratively) more about yourself.

FOR THE GUYS: If the night is ending and you or your love-interest had one too many cocktails and need to crash at your place, you'll score major points if you offer to sleep on the couch until your love-interest gives you the go-ahead to share a bed with you. It shows a level of chivalry and respect that is irresistible. Just offering to give your love-interest space shows that you are making an attempt to make her feel comfortable. Yes, she could take you up on the offer to sleep on the couch, but you're scoring major points with her even if things don't turn sexual that night.

THE SEX CONVERSATION

When you're getting to know your love-interest, a conversation about sex is recommended. These conversations can be difficult, but the trick is to make the conversation fun while keeping it casual and conversational. A flirty convo about your sexual preferences can be a turn-on in and of itself and can also serve as a way to see if you and your love-interest may be compatible. If things are starting to get sexual with your love-interest, these conversations are important to have to make sure you and your love-interest are on the same page sexually speaking. Here are a few questions to help you and your love-interest start your sex convo while also avoiding awkwardness, sexual frustration, or even anger in some cases.

- *Do you like being naked? How do you feel about nudity?*

- *Do you like to be more dominant or submissive sexually?*

- *What kind of protection do you prefer?*

- *Are you more traditional sexually speaking or are you more adventurous or unconventional? What makes this so?*

- *What turns you on? What turns you off?*

A WORD OF CAUTION: Try to avoid the 'how many people have you slept with' conversation. There is rarely anything good that can come out of a conversation where specific numbers and conquests are discussed. You're just asking for judgment, a comparing and contrasting of past partners and the like. Keep your sex conversation focused on the two of you. Ask the right questions and be clear about your boundaries. If your love-interest is truly interested in you, he or she will be open to answering your questions.

FOR THE LADIES: It's important to be aware of the signals you are sending to your love-interest. If you invite your date into your home, he may assume that it's an invitation for sex. If this is not an option for you, you may want to wait to invite your love-interest back to your place. Even if it's as simple as wanting to continue an amazing conversation you've been having, after the bars close, your love-interest may have a different interpretation of your invitation. To avoid any awkwardness, only invite your date into your home if you are okay with the possibility of him or her putting the moves on you. Remember you should always make the final decision as to what you want to participate in sexually, but it's also important not to send the wrong message to someone who is interested in you.

MAKING SURE YOU'RE ON THE SAME PAGE

If you plan on being intimate with your love-interest, it's important to discuss your sexual needs, wants, and desires. Never assume anything as far as sex is concerned. Your love-interest may only be interested in kissing or heavy petting during the early stage of courtship. Maybe your love-interest is only interested in sex...this is why the sex conversation is so important. If your boundaries are clear from the start, you will both be clear as to what will or won't happen at this stage in your relationship. If you are not okay with your partner's pace, he or she may not be the right person for you. If your love-interest wants to take things slow and you see potential for a relationship, be patient and respect your love-interest's boundaries. By making sure you are on the same page, you will establish a level of respect with your love-interest, which is a great basis for both short and long-term relationships.

SEX ISN'T THE ONLY OPTION

Often by default, singles assume that sex is the only way to express physical affection when it comes to dating and intimacy. Not true! Maybe you have chosen to abstain from intercourse or you only want to kiss or touch right now. There is no right or wrong choice here. Do only what you feel comfortable with and only with people who make you feel comfortable. This is why the sex conversation and making sure you're on the same page are so important. You may not want to announce your sexual boundaries when you first meet someone, but it's important when you want to get to know a new love-interest more intimately. Don't go on autopilot when it comes to sex. Consciously choose what you want to engage or not engage in sexually.

LOOK YOUR BEST SO YOU FEEL YOUR BEST

If you suspect that you and your love-interest may be heading towards something sexual, make sure you are prepared. There's nothing worse than an unexpected sexual encounter when you aren't properly (wo)manscaped. To be safe, make sure all intimate areas of the body are properly cleaned and groomed in case you and your love-interest get intimate.

Why add unnecessary anxiety into the equation by worrying about body odor or body hair? There's no need to go to the extreme, but making sure you have a neat appearance is a must. The objective is to drive your love-interest crazy, not drive them away.

SEXUAL SAFETY

You'll inevitably have moments when you'll connect with someone that you will want to be intimate with. When engaging in sexual activity, always practice safe sex. Whatever form of protection you use, make sure it's accessible during intimate moments. Don't rely on your partner to bring protection. Always have your own protection. It could be a clue to your partner's character if he or she isn't prepared or concerned about being safe sexually. If someone doesn't care about his or her own health, it's pretty safe to say that he or she may not be concerned about yours. Your health and your life are not worth one night of fun.

Being safe sexually also involves being emotionally and physically safe. Are you in a comfortable location with your partner? Do you feel safe with your partner? You should never engage in sexual activity with someone you don't feel comfortable with or in a place you aren't comfortable in. You are sharing your body, energy and spirit with someone new and that should always be done with someone you feel comfortable with and in a place that makes you feel safe. If you suddenly don't feel safe or comfortable, you have the right to change your mind about engaging in sexual activity before and even during a sexual encounter. If something doesn't feel right, you have the right to say 'NO' at any time.

FOR THE LADIES: As far as pregnancy is concerned, you are most fertile the days leading up to your period. A gal might want to take extra care during this time, by abstaining or using extra protection (condoms, spermicide, the pill, etc.) during sexual activity. If you do become pregnant and you want to discuss your options, seek advice from a medical professional ASAP, so you are able to consider all options available to you.

STDS AND PREVENTION

Sexually Transmitted Diseases (STDs) are a very real thing. Some can be cured and some cannot. Going back to the basics of 'Sex-Ed,' STDs can be transmitted through semen, blood and vaginal secretions. If you or your partner has a cut, cold sore, or abrasion on any body part that might come in contact with these bodily fluids, you must take extra care to be cautious when intimate. That means oral sex too. Though the chances are slim, you can pass or contract a STD through oral sex, not just through vaginal or anal sex.

It's also important to get annual checkups, including STD and HIV tests to protect yourself and others. Sometimes people don't realize that they're carrying an STD and so they might unknowingly pass it to you, which you could unknowingly pass on to someone else. This isn't meant to scare you, it's just a reminder that you are in control of your body and you should do everything in your power to protect yourself. If you have contracted an STD and you need help or advice, contact your doctor. There are a lot of non-profit organizations that offer free guidance and resources. Here are a few that could be of assistance.

Centers For Disease Control and Prevention
www.cdc.gov/sexualhealth

Planned Parenthood
www.plannedparenthood.com

Web M.D.
www.WedMD.com/sex-relationships

MAKING THE 1ST TIME SPECIAL

So you've had a great date or great few dates with your love-interest. There's definitely chemistry between the two of you and you think this could be the night that you two get to know each other more intimately. Remember that giving proper attention to your partner is extremely important. Do your best to be a generous intimate partner. Set the scene based on the likes and dislikes you've discussed during your sex conversation. For some people, a romantic scene with candles and soft music will be ideal. For others a totally dark room with techno music may be in order. Whatever his or her preference, make sure your partner feels comfortable. Your partner will appreciate any planning that was involved in setting up this encounter. You're ability to focus on your partner will make your connection stronger. Being distracted and not paying attention to your love-interest's sexual likes and dislikes will kill any romance. Listening to and observing your partner in the moment will teach you tons about what they like or don't like sexually. If the two of you aren't shy about the sex talk, keep the lines of communication open while exploring one another. This is a foolproof way to make sure both of you are enjoying the experience while fully engaged.

THE MORNING AFTER

At any rate, it's not polite to linger too long the morning after. Even if everything turned out great, if you are staying at his or her place, it's rude to hold your love-interest's day hostage by wearing out your welcome. It's a different story if he or she invites you to stay for breakfast or to hang out and get to know each other even better. If you're at your love-interest's place, let him or her invite you to stay longer. Otherwise, collect your things, collect yourself, thank him or her for a great night, suggest getting together again (assuming that's what you want) and be on your way.

FOR THE GUYS: If still interested, don't wait more than a few days to contact your love-interest after the first sexual encounter. If she likes you, she will be hoping to hear from you but she may also be a bit unsure about where things stand between the two of you. Play it cool, but not so cool that she loses interest. Stay on her radar!

FOR THE LADIES: Let him contact you after your first sexual encounter. This is also a test of his level of interest. If he's a gentleman, he'll thank you for a great evening. If he's interested, he'll also make plans to see you again. If he waits more than a week to call you after your sleepover, he's not that interested.

Have realistic expectations after an initial intimate encounter with someone new. Do not expect or assume that you are in a relationship just because you had sex. Remain as realistic as possible to have the best experience from beginning to end. Things could very well turn into a relationship, but it will probably be too early to tell what will happen between the two of you. Know what you are getting yourself into, so that you don't end up hating life when your rendezvous is over. There are a few different ways things could turn out with your love-interest. Here are a few reactions to look out for, so that you aren't caught off-guard after your sexy sleepover is complete.

FOR THE GUYS: How she could act after your intimate encounter

- *She might end up being possessive*

- *She might think she's in love with you*

- *She could expect the two of you to hang out constantly from here into the foreseeable future*

- *She might be cool with the whole situation and might not want anything more from you*

- *She might only want a sexual relationship with you*

FOR THE LADIES: How he could act after your intimate encounter

- *He might not call you again*

- *He might only call you for sex*

- *He might become less available and create some distance if he's afraid that you might get attached*

- *He might profess his love for you and you'll live happily ever after*

REDEEMING YOURSELF: MAKING A BAD 1ST TIME BETTER

So even though you prepared for potential awkwardness,

you had a frank, but fun sex conversation, and made your love-interest feel as comfortable as possible, there is still a chance that your first sexual experience may not have gone as well as you would have liked. Maybe you or your partner had to leave unexpectedly...Maybe there was an interruption...Maybe you were nervous and therefore you gave a lackluster sexual performance. The worst thing you can do when things don't go as planned, is act like nothing happened. Discuss the elephant in the room. It shows more confidence to discuss any weirdness that arose, especially if you bring it up in a fun way. Maybe you accidentally caused a sexually awkward moment...if so, it's your job to make future plans to hang with your love-interest to make things right. Don't let too much time go by before scheduling another attempt. Don't let the awkwardness fester for too long. Be timely with your efforts to redeem yourself. After a follow up date is made, do everything you can do to make sure the same thing doesn't happen. If you had to get up early for work the first time, make plans on a night when your schedule is less of an issue. If there was an interruption, plan your rendezvous in an environment where there will be no distractions. If things weren't functioning normally physically, do what you can to prepare yourself physically. Learn from the first awkward experience and do everything you can to avoid history repeating itself. Above all, don't avoid another attempt. Your love-interest might think that it was his or her fault or that you are no longer interested. Confirm your interest by making another date.

JUST A HOOKUP OR SOMETHING MORE?

After an early sexual experience with a new love-interest, it's easy to hypothesize, overanalyze, and speculate what our new love-interest is thinking about us, feeling for us, wanting from us, and potentially doing with others. It can be difficult to go with the flow, which can make it hard to successfully navigate an early hookup situation with a new love-interest. Consider having a brief and light conversation with your love-interest in regards to what you are looking for now that the sexual barrier has been crossed. Are you both only interested in a physical relationship? Is one of you only interested in a serious relationship? There is no right or wrong answer here, it's just a matter of figuring out if the two of you are on the same page.

It is possible to build a relationship from a brief encounter, but it can sometimes be difficult to get out of the 'hookup mindset' and see each other as more than just a good time. It's not impossible to transition into a relationship after an early hookup, but both you and your love-interest have to be on the same page emotionally, physically, and possibly even spiritually. If you've chosen your love-interest wisely and had an informative but fun sex conversation, there's a good chance that your dating and relationship goals will be equally matched.

DEALING WITH REJECTION AFTER SEX

If a week has gone by after your rendezvous, and you haven't received a call or your call wasn't returned, it's best to continue with your dating life without him or her. You may hear from him or her again, but don't put your life on hold waiting for him or her to call. For whatever reason, he or she is not interested in continuing or starting a relationship. If this happens, just let it go. Any 'rejection' that happens early on in new relationships is a blessing. It's better to know someone's level of interest earlier rather than later, before lots of time and energy has been invested. Don't swear off dating just because things ended in a way that you didn't expect. Don't let one experience with one person determine your entire dating life.

CHAPTER 9

CAUTION! RED FLAGS AHEAD

Everyone you accept into your dating life should meet a reasonable set of standards. Dealbreakers are those standards a love-interest doesn't meet that stop you from getting more serious. Dealbreakers are warning signs that someone needs to work on themselves before being with you. Overlooking these signs could be harmful physically, mentally, or emotionally. No one should ever make you feel enraged, powerless, or worthless. Don't waste your time with someone that lowers your self-image or makes you unhappy. You can't control who you're attracted to, but you can choose to walk away from a potentially damaging situation.

Even though you may not be looking for 'The One' right now, you should still choose your short-term partners carefully. Your potential love-interests and partners should meet your relationship goals and dating objectives. Yes, you may be left with a smaller pool of options, but *quality* is better than *quantity*, especially when it comes to dating. Here's a list of communication, emotional, lifestyle, and physical dealbreakers you should look out for when getting to know a new love-interest.

COMMUNICATION WARNINGS

IF HE OR SHE...

1. TELLS YOU TO 'SHUT UP' DURING A CONVERSATION

Verbal abuse is still abuse and someone trying to silence you literally or figuratively is abusive behavior. Be wary of anyone that won't let you express yourself or tries to stop you from sharing your opinion or communicating in general. It's a sure sign of disrespect and nothing good can come from that.

2. BELITTLES YOU OR SOMETHING YOU'RE DOING OR ACCOMPLISHING

A relationship should be about supporting each other's dreams. You want people in your life who are going to encourage and support you. Anyone who makes you feel bad about achievements and accomplishments is no good for you.

3. NEVER COMPLIMENTS YOU

Especially in the early months, you should be showing your appreciation for each other. Giving genuine compliments should be a natural part of an exciting new relationship. Make sure that your love-interest isn't in an exclusive relationship with themselves.

4. COMPLAINS ABOUT SPENDING TOO MUCH MONEY ON YOU (ESPECIALLY IF NO REAL MONEY HAS BEEN SPENT) OR IF HE OR SHE MAKES YOU FEEL GUILTY ABOUT THE MONEY HE OR SHE SPENDS ON YOU

No one should ever make you feel guilty for being taken out. Your date made the decision to ask you out and pay for the date, therefore he or she should be prepared to pay. It is your decision whether or not you actually let them pay or if you make a contribution to the bill. Having said that, if anyone gets angry with you for accepting their offer to pay, it might be time to leave them with the bill and without a date.

5. IS RUDE TO YOUR FRIENDS OR FAMILY

No way! Your friends and family are an extension of you and your date should show them respect just knowing that they are connected to you. One exception to this dealbreaker is if your friend or family has directly insulted your date and your date is simply sticking up for him or herself. Even in that special case, your date should do everything possible to make a good impression.

6. DOESN'T LISTEN TO YOU OR YOUR CONCERNS OR TAKE YOU SERIOUSLY

If your love-interest has no interest in hearing your feelings or concerns about a situation, that should be a clear sign to you that your partner is not willing or able to hear you. Having a romantic partner is one of the most intimate relationships you will have in your life. It's important that you are able to express important things with him or her and if you are unable or discouraged from doing that, you are robbing yourself and your partner from a healthy, happy relationship and possibly damaging your self-worth in the process.

7. MAKES DEROGATORY COMMENTS ABOUT YOUR RACE, ETHNICITY, OR CULTURAL BACKGROUND

Your love-interest should accept you for you! You should not have to defend who you are to them or anyone else. Either they respect you, your culture, and where you come from, or they don't. Relationships are built on respect and if there is no respect for something as basic as your background, a respectful relationship cannot be built.

8. IS TOO PROUD TO SAY THEY'RE SORRY

We all make mistakes, but some of us have trouble admitting when we've made them. You can tell someone's character by the way they handle themselves in sensitive situations.

9. NEVER ASKS YOU QUESTIONS ABOUT YOURSELF

Dating is about getting to know someone. If your love-interest isn't making an attempt to ask the right questions and get to know you, this person may not be interested. You may be thinking, "but my love-interest is on a date with me...of course they are interested in me." Maybe not. He or she might just want to find someone that they can impress or someone who wants to hear all about them. Your love-interest should want to know all about you. There should be a natural give-and-take in terms of conversation and interest in one another and a genuine desire to find out about your life, wants, needs and desires.

10. DOESN'T STICK UP FOR YOU

We aren't necessarily talking physical battles, but we are talking about your love-interest being on your team instead of leaving you to fight on your own. For example, if his or her friends were making fun of you, you'd want your love-interest to tell them to cut it out rather than join in on the belittling. You want to be with someone that will have your back in an awkward situation, not leave you hanging.

11. SAYS, "I'D NEVER HIT SOMEONE I LOVE, BUT..."

There should never be a 'but' in that sentence... there is no excuse that justifies hitting someone you care about. If your love-interest has ever used this phrase, be grateful they're showing you their boundaries so early in the relationship, before things get too serious. Statements like these should be taken very seriously.

EMOTIONAL WARNINGS

IF HE OR SHE....

12. HAS AN ALL CONSUMING HATE FOR AN EX

We've all had a tough time in a breakup, but eventually the healthy thing to do is to let go. If your love-interest still has an intense hatred for his or her ex, that is a big dealbreaker. Not being able to let go of a situation is a warning sign that someone isn't able to cope with disappointment. Especially if your love-interest is vengeful, has threatened an ex or spends their life making their ex's life miserable, that's a huge warning sign. You don't want any part of that negativity making its way into your life!

13. IS DEPRESSIVE OR GENERALLY UNHAPPY

Negative energy is contagious. If you are someone who is generally happy and positive, be cautious about being with someone who is depressive and hates life. That mindset will only bring you down!

14. HAS AN UNHEALTHY JEALOUSY OF YOU OR ANYTHING IN YOUR LIFE

Your love-interest and potential partner should be supportive and encouraging of you, not jealous of your accomplishments, including career or income. Especially for the ladies, your guy should be excited about your endeavors. Anyone who sees that as a threat is not the one for you.

15. DOESN'T LIKE THEMSELVES OR HAS LOW SELF-ESTEEM

This is the source of so many issues in relationships. If your love-interest is not happy with themselves, they are bound to make everyone around them miserable too. A relationship with someone who doesn't like him or herself is excruciating. You'll constantly be trying to make your love-interest happy, which is a losing battle. True self worth and happiness come from within.

16. CRITICIZES YOU FOR NOT GOING TO THE GYM OR CALLS YOU FAT

Even if you are carrying a few extra pounds, there is a supportive way to suggest someone get in shape. If your love-interest makes you feel bad about yourself, calls you names or treats you disrespectfully based on your weight or your appearance in general, it's time to get away. You need support, not criticism.

17. MAKES YOU FEEL UNWORTHY OR LESS CONFIDENT

Choose a love-interest that makes you happy to be you! Even if your love-interest does everything possible to make you feel good about yourself, it doesn't matter if you still don't feel worthy. Only choose to be in relationships with people that you feel good around, that you feel confident around, and who you can be yourself with. Whether self-inflicted or induced by your love-interest…you should never feel unworthy around your love-interest.

18. PICKS FIGHTS WITH YOU OR THREATENS YOU

Fighting takes a lot of energy and you should not waste your energy on negativity, especially when that negativity is directed at you. People who are constantly in conflict with others are not happy within themselves. Especially in the early months, your relationship with your love-interest should be easy, fun and based on mutual respect. You should never feel emotionally threatened.

19. MAKES YOU FEEL UNCOMFORTABLE BEING YOURSELF

You should be able to be yourself around your love-interest. It takes a lot of time and energy to keep up a façade like this. A relationship based on dishonesty is sure to fail. If you aren't honest about who you really are for fear that your love-interest will reject you, consider that your love-interest will discover the 'real' you at some point, so why not just get honest? Be honest with yourself. Are you happy not being yourself around someone you are potentially building a relationship with? There is no greater freedom than to be who you really are around people you care about. And if your love-interest doesn't like the real you, let him or her go and make room for someone who thinks the real you is fantastic.

20. MAKES YOUR FEEL UNCOMFORTABLE, UNEASY, SCARED OR SUSPICIOUS AROUND HIM OR HER

This is your intuition speaking to you! Maybe they've given you a reason to feel suspicious or uneasy...maybe not. Maybe it's just a feeling you are getting. Go with that feeling. It might not be rational and it doesn't have to be. Even if your love-interest is a good person with no tricks up their sleeve, if you are uncomfortable, that is not someone you should be with. A healthy relationship cannot exist where there is fear, suspicion, and uneasiness.

21. TELLS YOU THAT YOUR CONFIDENCE MAKES HIM OR HER FEEL LESS CONFIDENT OR ENCOURAGES YOU TO BE LESS CONFIDENT TO BOOST THEIR CONFIDENCE

Nope. Not okay! Your confidence should not affect anyone that chooses to be with you. If you are confident, stay that way. If someone has a problem with your confidence, you are not the person for them. You should never have to give up self-confidence in order to be with someone. NEVER! If your confidence makes someone feel bad about themselves, that is not your problem... it's theirs!!

22. MAKES YOU UNHAPPY MORE THAN YOU ARE HAPPY

This should also be a no-brainer, but sometimes we need a gentle reminder. We are so focused on a specific goal, that we forget that we should be dating people that make us happy. A love-interest should never add to your stress level.

LIFESTYLE WARNINGS

IF HE OR SHE...

23. IS TOO BUSY TO SEE YOU

Part of dating is spending time with someone. If your love-interest is never available, or isn't available as much as you'd like, a relationship may not be in the cards. We make time for people we really want in our lives, especially people we're considering being intimate with. If you aren't spending quality time together regularly, it may be time to move on.

24. IS EXTREMELY INDECISIVE

Being successful in life is to make choices and

stand by those choices. If your date finds it hard to make decisions even about small things, that could be a bad sign of things to come.

25. TAKES MAJOR RISKS WITH THEIR FINANCES

Let's face it. A lot of us have some amount of financial debt. There's a difference between someone who is trying to get out of debt and someone who is steadily adding to it and doesn't have a plan to get out of it. You want to be with someone that is making an effort to do what they can to make their situation better...not someone who wallows in self-pity or blames everyone else for their situation.

26. DOESN'T HAVE A PLAN FOR THE FUTURE

We may choose different things in life. What we thought we wanted to do in our 20s, may not be what we want to do in our 30s and beyond. This is totally normal. It becomes a problem when your love-interest hasn't thought at all about their future and doesn't have a plan (even a vague plan) for what's to come in their life. They may be figuring things out, but there should be at least a thought about the direction their life is headed. Drifters need not apply!

27. DOESN'T KEEP THEIR WORD

This is a big one! Keeping one's word shows a level of honor and integrity. Someone keeping their word forms a foundation for trust. Being on time for dates and following through with scheduled dates are examples of keeping your word in a dating scenario. If your love-interest cannot be counted on or breaks simple promises early on, it could be a bad sign of things to come.

28. DOESN'T TAKE THEIR TIME WITH YOU OR RUSHES THROUGH DATES OR MEETINGS WITH YOU

Being with you should be a treat and a pleasure. Be cautious if someone doesn't want to take the time to get to know you and spend time with you. Dating is about getting to know someone and spending time with them. If your love-interest doesn't make time or have the desire to see you on a regular basis, find someone who does. Life's too short to spend with someone who doesn't really want to be with you.

29. NEVER ASKS YOU TO SPEND THE NIGHT AT THEIR PLACE OR NEVER WANTS TO SLEEP AT YOUR PLACE

If you have hit the point with your love-interest where you are becoming intimate and he or she never invites you to spend the night, they may be hiding something from you. They may not be hiding a spouse, boyfriend, or girlfriend, but there may be something that they don't want you seeing at their place. If the two of you are becoming close, you may just want to suggest to them politely, "Hey! I'd love to see your place sometime." A simple comment like that could prompt a conversation or at least an explanation as to why you haven't been invited over. Before moving forward in the relationship, make sure you get to see their place and possibly find out what all the secrecy is about.

30. TRIES TO CHANGE YOU IN A DRASTIC WAY

We're not talking about a love-interest encouraging you to keep your apartment neat and tidy…we're talking about your love-interest trying to change who you are as a person. If someone wants to date you, they should be dating YOU, not dating you to change you into someone else. If they want to date someone else, let them date someone else!

31. ONLY LOOKS OUT FOR THEMSELVES

If your love-interest is totally self-involved and has no concern for your happiness, safety, or wellbeing, it's time to get out while you can. Dating and relationships are about sharing experiences and looking out for each other. When dating, especially if things are progressing towards exclusivity, you should be looking out for each other's best interests.

32. DOESN'T AT LEAST OFFER TO HELP YOU EMOTIONALLY, PHYSICALLY, OR FINANCIALLY IF YOU ARE STRUGGLING WITH SOMETHING

We aren't talking indefinite support here. We're talking offering temporary help to someone you care about. There should be a desire to at least offer assistance. You might not feel comfortable or it might not be appropriate to accept your love-interest's offer, but there should at least be an offer, a suggestion or the offering of a resource that could help you make your situation better. If your love-interest couldn't care less about your predicament, it might be time to care less about him or her.

33. PUTS OFF SEEING YOU

Everyone's busy, but if it seems like your love-interest always has something better to do or plans things with you only when other plans have fallen through or once he or she knows everyone else's status, your instincts might be right on. Don't be second best! If you don't mind a last minute date-night scenario, you can at least ask for respect within the spontaneity. For example, you can tell your love-interest a time that you will no longer be available to accept a date, which gives him/her a set of parameters to work within. A blatant disrespect for your schedule is never acceptable.

34. RARELY CALLS YOU OR CONTACTS YOU

This goes along with the previous dealbreaker. Sure one person might call the other more, but both parties should be making an effort to communicate and get together. If you are making all of the effort all of the time, it might be time to find someone who can't wait to initiate contact with you.

35. DOESN'T WANT TO GET INTIMATE WITH YOU OR DOESN'T MAKE AN ATTEMPT TO SHOW YOU AFFECTION

When both of you feel ready, there should be some level of intimacy shared between you and your love-interest. This does not necessarily mean sex or anything sexual, but simple gestures of affection, which could be as basic as kissing or handholding. If your love-interest isn't interested in sharing energy or affection with you, maybe you should encourage them or better yet, initiate small gestures of affection to get the ball rolling. If he or she doesn't respond positively, it might be an indicator that they might not feel the same way about you that you feel about them.

36. STILL LIVES WITH THEIR PARENTS

This might not apply in different cultures and religions. In many countries in Europe, it is more accepted to live at your parents' home until you are in a committed relationship or married. In the US, generally speaking, it might be a bit odd to have never lived on your own or with a roommate. There are of course exceptions. We're not talking about someone who has had to move back into their parents' house for financial reasons for example. If there's never been an attempt to live on their own, this could mean that your love-interest may not have fully embraced adulthood.

37. CAN'T STAND ANY SORT OF CHANGE, INCLUDING CHANGES YOU MAY MAKE TO YOURSELF

Maybe you are on a spiritual journey…maybe you've decided to get a degree…if your love-interest tries to stop these changes that will make you better, it might be time to make yourself better by distancing yourself from him or her. Your love interest should encourage your growth. Any discouragement of you bettering yourself is fear on their part that you may make yourself better and leave them behind. Encourage them to join you on your journey of growth. If they aren't interested in your self-improvement or change for the better, it might be time to continue your growth without them.

38. HIDES SOMEONE SPECIAL IN THEIR LIFE FROM YOU

If you are starting to become serious with your love-interest, then you are probably starting to meet his or her friends. Is there a guy or girl that you know is close with your love-interest that you have yet to meet officially? Why would someone you're getting to know consciously choose not introduce you to someone else in their life? It may be innocent, but especially if it's one specific person that your love-interest brings up regularly, it seems normal for them to want you to meet each other…unless there is something to hide. Ask to arrange a group hang session to meet this mysterious friend. It's not your place to demand to be introduced to everyone in your love-interest's life when you're still getting to know each other, but if there seems to be intense avoidance of making an introduction, there could be cause for concern.

39. DOESN'T KNOW CURRENT EVENTS

These days it's simply irresponsible to not be informed about general world events. Your love-interest doesn't need to be doing live reports on CNN or anything, but it's important to know something about the world. Being informed about news, current events, politics, trends, etc. will make your conversations that much more interesting.

40. WON'T TAKE NO FOR AN ANSWER

No means no! We're not just talking sex here... regardless of the request, if you aren't interested; you have the right to say NO! If your love-interest doesn't respect your boundaries, they are not respecting you and a lack of respect for you should never be acceptable.

41. DISAPPROVES OF SOMETHING YOU'VE DONE IN THE PAST

If your love-interest can't get over something from your past, it might be time to get over them. The past is in the past. If he or she disapproves of things you did before the two of you met, they may subtly be punishing you for those past decisions. We learn from our mistakes and you are moving forward with life. If they can't move forward, it might be time to move on to someone who can see you for who you are today…not punish you for who you were in the past.

PHYSICAL WARNINGS

IF HE OR SHE…

42. TAKES RISKS REGARDING YOUR SAFETY

Definitely not okay! Your date should be on their best behavior in the early months of dating and that means keeping you out of harm's way to the best of their ability. It's about making a good first impression and not getting your date into a dangerous situation.

43. WON'T LET YOU SEE THEIR BODY

This one is applies to relationships that are becoming a bit more intimate. Maybe you've already had a few make-out sessions, but things seem to stop at a certain point, or things continue, but with odd clothing on. It is possible that your love-interest is embarrassed about their body or hiding something. Avoid making them feel bad, but you should definitely ask them about their shyness. If you are to the point where you are intimate, you have a right to see the body in which you are sharing that intimacy…that is a legitimate request!

44. FORCES YOU TO DO ANYTHING SEXUAL THAT YOU AREN'T COMFORTABLE WITH

Intimacy and sex should be consensual. Don't let anyone guilt you into being sexual, which can be anything from a kiss, to sex. It's your body and you decide who to share it with. Guilt or coercion should never be part of the equation.

45. HITS, PUSHES, SHOVES, OR SLAPS YOU

Even if you don't have a red flag list, this should be reason to breakup #1. No one should ever put their hands on you without your consent. It is NEVER okay for someone to use force against you, especially someone that 'cares' about you. Even if you are having an argument, it should not turn into anything physical. This goes for men too. It is not okay for anyone you're in a relationship with to get physical with you!

Your 'dealbreakers' list will help you set boundaries with everyone in your life. It doesn't have to be an actual list on paper, nor should you adopt everything on this list. Once you are consciously choosing and rejecting certain behaviors, energies, and people, you will also consciously choose to effectively take control of your dating life. Even if someone in your life is making an effort to change certain behaviors, their effort may not be good enough for you. That's when you make the choice to lower your standards a bit (only if they are unrealistically high) or call it quits. Make your own list of dealbreakers to help you get clear about setting your own relationship boundaries.

FOLLOWING YOUR INTUITION

We sometimes get gut feelings about people, but we choose to ignore them because we feel other things are more important, like how much a guy earns or what a girl looks like, for example. Yes, these things do hold some significance, but by focusing on superficial traits, we can sometimes overlook a person's inner qualities. Pay attention! People give you clues about their 'true self' pretty early on. Following your intuition will help you to make the right choices. It's there to protect you! Maybe your love-interest really wants to change for the better, but his or her 'better' might not be good enough for you. This doesn't mean that they are a terrible person; it just means that you need more than they can give you. It doesn't make you a jerk to have standards, it just means that you know what you want...and don't want in a relationship.

CHAPTER 10

THE FAT LADY HAS SUNG!

In both short and long-term relationships, there will be breakups! Once you accept this as part of the dating process, it becomes much easier. Not every couple is meant to last forever...that does not mean that a relationship didn't mean anything...it simply means that it has run its course. Breakups are made better or worse depending on how the breakup is actually carried out and how each party chooses to react to the breakup. Ultimately it's important to keep your emotions under control in these tough situations. When we react before thinking our actions through, things can get ugly.

Whether you were blindsided by your love-interest ending things prematurely or you've simply decided that a new relationship just isn't for you for one reason or another, you and your partner are breaking up for a reason. Something wasn't working for one or both of you and that is reason enough to let the relationship go and be open to new and more positive possibilities. Here are some things to remember when going through a breakup with someone new:

THE BREAKING POINT

You'll know when you've hit your breaking point in a new relationship because your love-interest will do or say something that will immediately make you want to end the new relationship. Maybe he or she has become aggressive. Maybe you realize you have nothing in common. You've hit your breaking point when something shifts in you that makes you lose interest in being with your love-interest. They say love is blind because oftentimes you are so in love, like, or lust that you don't notice what's really going on. You have feelings for your love-interest that color your objectivity and decision-making skills. Once the veil of love or lust has been lifted and you are able to see the facts of your relationship, you may not like what remains.

Sometimes being honest with yourself means ending a relationship that has run its course or where you are no longer working things out constructively or being emotionally supportive of each other. You should be making each other better and having fun together, especially in the early months.

Sometimes the end of a relationship is not so definite. That's when it takes more strength to know when to call it quits in your relationship. Your partner might not be strong enough to end things permanently or maybe you've broken up and gotten back together so many times that you don't know exactly what's happening. This is when you may need to be the one walk away.

You may also hit your breaking point while trying to 'fix' someone. You can always encourage your love-interest's growth but there is a fine line between encouragement and enabling. You can be of support, but if someone has deep emotional issues or is struggling with addiction, you are most likely not equipped to help them in the way that they need help, especially early on in a relationship. Support them as a friend, but recognize that...

- *Your love-interest needs to help themselves before you can offer help to them. You can only offer suggestions to help them improve their situation. If they aren't ready to initiate change in their own life, the support you offer will only help them minimally.*

- *If you try to 'fix' them, it could end up hurting you. In some cases, you may not be equipped to handle a situation your love-interest is dealing with and 'fixing' them can take your happiness and deplete your energy.*

- *Enabling someone you care about can do more harm than good. Old patterns could stay the same and things may never change. Your love-interest will feel supported with you there, but it may not be a healthy support that benefits both of you.*

THE BREAKUP CONVERSATION

Let's face it, breaking up with a love-interest is never fun, but you can lessen the drama by ending things in a classy way. If you've only been dating someone for a few months, you shouldn't have to go through a long breakup process like you might in a long-term relationship. But be sensitive to the fact that your love-interest may really like you and this breakup may have totally caught him or her off guard.

If you want to lessen your chances of looking like the bad guy or girl, here are a few tips for avoiding a drama-filled break up.

1. AVOID BREAKING UP ELECTRONICALLY

Ignoring your love-interest altogether would be more polite than breaking up via text, email or social media message. Choose to handle your breakup like an adult. Call your former love-interest to tell him or her the truth or maybe you'd prefer to tell them face-to-face. Rest assured that if you ignore your love-interest he or she will contact you to see why you've disappeared. Be prepared that a breakup conversation will most likely happen whether or not you choose to initiate it.

2. TRY TO BE RESPECTFULLY HONEST AS TO WHY YOU'RE ENDING THINGS

Maybe you see your love-interest as a friend more than a potential partner or maybe you just aren't looking for a serious relationship. Most people will understand these reasons for ending a new relationship. He or she might still be upset, but if he or she understands why you're ending things, it may be easier for them to handle.

3. BE NICE .

Unnecessary breakup reasons can hurt feelings…. keep things general. If you don't feel any chemistry with a love-interest, you've met someone new, or you just aren't that into dating him or her, there's no need to announce it. If you can't say anything nice, don't say anything at all.

If you really like your ex love-interest, suggest continuing a friendship, but only if you sincerely want to be friends. Just because you didn't work out romantically doesn't mean that you can't hang out with each other if you both want to. The two of you may be better friends than you could have ever been as partners.

A breakup is never easy, but if you treat your ex love-interest with respect it will make the process less dramatic. Your ex love-interest will be sad to hear that your new relationship is coming to an end, but your classiness will help to ease his or her heartache.

AVOIDING CONFLICT DURING A BREAKUP

There are times when a love-interest won't understand where you're coming from, why you broke it off with them, or why it's time for you to move on. In cases like this, it's better to avoid an extended discussion that will surely end where it began...in 'confusion-misunderstanding-land.' When you feel like conversations about the relationship have stopped being productive and may be starting to turn negative or even argumentative, it may be time to end the discussion once and for all. Rather than beat a dead horse simply try the following strategies to end a never-ending breakup conversation:

1. CHANGE THE SUBJECT

Avoid talking about the subjects you can't get past or the things the two of you can't agree on. When you realize that you can't see eye to eye, sometimes the only thing you can do is to let go of your ego, stop the debating, and start talking about something else altogether. Don't keep revisiting the same conversation if you keep getting the same result. If he or she doesn't understand where you are coming from, and you've tried repeatedly to get through to them, it may be time to face the fact that you may never see eye to eye. Keep the convo light and non-confrontational because sometimes an ex will try and make you angry on purpose just to make you unhappy or to get what they want. If you remain cool, calm, and collected, you will more easily avoid breakup drama.

2. AGREE WITH YOUR EX

Maybe your ex is accusing you of something that you didn't do. Rather than have the same 'no I didn't' convo for the 10th time, simply agree with them. It's a bit of a Jedi mind trick. Yes, it can be hard to take the blame, especially when something wasn't your fault, but in a reverse psychology sort-of-way, agreeing with your ex will end an impending argument. Once you agree that they're right and you're wrong, there will be nothing else to argue about.

3. AVOID YOUR EX ALTOGETHER

This should be a last resort. Don't burn bridges unless something extreme has happened. If he or she refuses to even try to see where you are coming from, or he or she keeps bringing up new things to argue about or blame you for, it might be best to totally disappear from each others' lives. If nothing constructive is happening or one of you can't let go of the past, it may be best to end things completely. Sometimes relationships don't work out and sometimes people we love need room to heal on their own. Let him or her work through their issues without your interference, so you can have space to work on yourself.

ANGER AND RESENTMENT AFTER A BREAKUP

It is normal to feel angry, bitter, or resentful after a breakup. You may feel angry because you weren't ready for the relationship to end or because of how the relationship ended. You may feel angry or resentful because you have to start the dating process all over again. These are all normal things to feel during and after a breakup. Allow yourself some time to feel angry. If you don't allow yourself to feel these emotions, you won't heal properly. Take some time to experience these feelings, but don't let them become your permanent way of being. Anger, bitterness, and other negative emotions will eat away at you if you fail to deal with them in a timely matter. Make an effort not to stay in this low energy place for too long. Keep things in perspective and pull yourself (or have friends pull you) out of this dark place when the time is right.

Let's put your situation into perspective. Just because the two of you didn't work out, it doesn't mean that your ex was the only person in the world for you. Breakups always happen for a reason, not by accident. Generally speaking, breakups will only add to your growth both as a person and as a future partner if you choose to learn from them.

GRUDGES ONLY HURT YOU

After a reasonable amount of time has passed, it's important to let go of your ex-focused anger. You may think that getting even or pretending he or she doesn't exist will teach your ex a lesson, but in reality it only hurts you! When you hold on to anger or resentment and attempt to direct it at someone, it's really only directed at you because it takes energy to hate. It's taking YOUR energy to hate your ex. That is energy and time that could be used creating new experiences and forming new bonds with new people. Leave the past in the past. It cannot be changed. It doesn't deserve any more of your attention. Don't give your ex the indirect power of still having influence over how you live your life. If you keep reliving that drama over and over, it will physically, emotionally, and spiritually take its toll on you again and again as if it was happening in real time. Focus on the present. The quicker you can let go of your ex and what happened between the two of you, the quicker you will be able to get on with life and start meeting singles that are better suited to you.

SADNESS AND DEPRESSION

Even if your breakup is for the best, it still hurts. It's a loss. The loss of a relationship. And where there is loss, there is sadness. Depending on the duration and intensity of the relationship, your sadness can turn into symptoms of depression. Do what you can to avoid getting stuck in that phase indefinitely. This breakup is not the end of the world and it certainly isn't the end of your life. Mourn for a respectable amount of time then choose to move on. Seek professional help if necessary. Don't let the end of a relationship end you! Your ex is out there living his or her life post-breakup and so should you! There are plenty of fish in the sea!

Of course you'll wonder if your ex is hurting as bad as you are hurting. Rest assured that unless your ex love-interest is unfeeling, and heartless, they will be hurting too. People express their sadness in different ways. Some isolate themselves while others seek comfort in the arms of others. That does not mean that they don't feel badly about what has happened. They have simply chosen a specific way to deal with their pain.

FORGIVING AND FORGETTING

If you've hurt someone and he or she cannot accept your apology, you may just have to come to terms with that. Depending on the offense, it may take your love-interest weeks or months to forgive you. You may have to face the fact that he or she may never forgive you. All you can do is make it known that you are sorry, acknowledge that your actions were unacceptable, do what you can to make amends and hope that your love-interest will eventually get over what happened. Even if you did something horrible in your relationship, you don't deserve to be in a relationship where your partner cannot forgive you and punishes you because of your misbehavior. You may have been in the wrong, but if your love-interest can't accept your apology after a reasonable amount of time, you'll have to face the fact that the damage may have been done and the relationship may be irreparable. If your partner is unable to forgive, it may be time to go your separate ways.

If after several attempts to reconcile, your love-interest decides to leave the relationship, let him or her leave. You've apologized, you've made changes, you've presented your arguments and he or she has made their choice. You should never have to beg someone to love you. Mourn the loss or the relationship, learn from your mistakes, and make room for someone new.

A WORD OF CAUTION ABOUT DRUGS AND ALCOHOL

Alcohol, drugs and sex are crutches that we sometimes cling to in tough times. Be careful. Using substances to cope can lead to more serious issues. These things might 'solve' your problems temporarily, but not in the long term. If your use turns to abuse and you need assistance, seek professional help. There is no shame in getting help dealing with an addiction. Here are a few organizations that can help.

Alcoholics Anonymous
www.AA.org

Drug Rehab Center
www.DrugRehabCenter.com
800-559-9503

The Betty Ford Center
www.BettyFordCenter.org
800-434-7518

BREAKUP PEP TALK

Breakups are never fun. Just like dealing with any sort of loss, you will grieve, heal, and eventually move past the hurt to where it's a distant memory. Here are some things to remember when you're in the middle of the breakup process and finding it hard to get over an ex:

- *Remember your new ex's faults. Nobody's perfect, and your ex is your ex for a reason. Remembering your ex's faults will help you to move on.*

- *Remind yourself that you shouldn't be with someone that makes you feel bad about yourself, doesn't respect you, your opinions, your feelings or doesn't want to be with you. You deserve better!*

- *Remind yourself that this too shall pass. You've lived through breakups before and you will get through this one too.*

- *Realize that this is a new beginning and that breakups happen for a significant reason. Your ex has just made room for something bigger and better to enter into your life. One door closes, another door opens.*

- *Remind yourself that you were still getting to know your ex love-interest. Just think about how much harder this breakup would have been if you had gotten really attached to him or her after dating for several months or even years.*

BECOMING FRIENDS AFTER A BREAKUP

Just because you and your love-interest didn't work out, it doesn't mean that you have to hate their guts; it just means that you weren't the right match for each other. Why do you have to be enemies? You liked or even loved something about each other at one point in time. If you want to be friends or at least friendly with an ex, it's important to focus on those things. You will have to let go of your ego to accomplish this. Being friends does not mean that you will have the same feelings you had for each other before. It's simply about letting go of what you were and embracing a new friendship. This 'being friends' strategy is for those special exs that you connected with and still care about. It is a gift to be able to catch up and share things that have happened in your lives and be genuinely happy to see each other and celebrate each other's successes and new relationships.

This is not a strategy for winning back an ex. This plan is for either 'friendship use' or quite simply for avoiding awkwardness if by chance you run into each other in town. To become friends you will need to let go of the baggage that you gained during the hard times together. Of course, you may never forget the bad times, but this is about forgiving, letting go of negativity, and allowing good energy to flow in all aspects of your life. It's also about understanding that you are both human beings that are capable of making mistakes from time to time, but that doesn't turn someone you used to care about into the scum of the Earth.

First and foremost, you must let go of the past, accept that the two of you are not meant to be in a relationship, and really be okay with that. You will need a healing period for this to work. To heal effectively means not having ANY communication with that person. You need time to sort out what happened between the two of you on your own. This of course takes time. After a breakup, it could take anywhere from a few months to a year of distance before trying to be friends depending on the length of the relationship and the intensity of the breakup.

Secondly, after you've had sufficient time away from each other, one of you will probably decide to contact the other just to check-in and say *hello*. There must be an equal amount of effort for this to work though. If you reach out initially, holidays, birthdays and special occasions are good excuses to contact an ex or someone you want to reconnect with. Who doesn't like a 'Happy Birthday', 'Congratulations', or 'Happy New Year?!' This is when a new FRIENDSHIP can develop. Be prepared that your ex may be surprised to hear from you and may not know what to say. Just be honest and tell them that they popped into your head and you wanted to say hello. Because it's rare to find people who are able to express themselves in a positive way after a breakup, your gesture of friendship will be appreciated. You may need to give them some time to process the fact that you've reappeared. After the initial shock, you can casually suggest a friendly coffee sometime. Their reaction will tell you if they have any interest in a friendship. No matter the outcome, your maturity and sensitivity will not go unnoticed.

Thirdly, the key at this stage is to be respectful, rational, and remain in the present. Respect is an absolute must! There are most likely hurt feelings on both sides. Let it go! Be nice to each other and give each other the respect that you would give any other friend, colleague, or acquaintance. Your ex will almost certainly be impressed by your maturity and be touched to know that you care and will possibly show you their tender side in the process.

If your ex doesn't accept your invitation for friendship, move on. Sometimes exs just can't be friends. He or she has their reasons. Maybe you hurt them worse than you thought. Maybe he or she is married and their new spouse wouldn't like the idea. Maybe they just don't want to revisit past feelings. Maybe your ex still has feelings for you. Sometimes it's harder to be friends if someone's ego was bruised in the breakup process. Once some time has passed and you've both dated other people and moved on with life, it can be easier to start a friendship. If friendship is not possible, accept their decision and move on knowing that you made an effort and tried to make things right with them. Move on with your life. Don't take it personally!

SUPPORTING A LOVED ONE GOING THROUGH A BREAKUP

It takes some people a few months, some a few years, and others a lifetime to reach their breaking point or see the truth in their relationship. Everyone processes a breakup in their own time and in their own way. As a friend or family member, you can be a shoulder to cry on and that's really all you can do. If you are too vocal about a loved one's relationship, your loved one might rebel against you instead of their love-interest. Being a good friend or loved one is to bring these things up, but not get angry if that person doesn't take your advice and end their relationship immediately after talking with you. They are learning an important lesson in their own time. You may be the only one they feel they can confide in, so be gentle, voice your concern, but don't get angry or abandon them. If they are in an abusive situation, it may be necessary to seek or suggest professional assistance. Here are a few resources.

The Hotline (National Domestic Violence Hotline)
1-800-799-SAFE (7233)
www.TheHotline.org

Know The Signs (Suicide Prevention Resource)
1-800-273-8255
www.suicideispreventable.org

ACCEPTANCE

A day will come where you will be okay with the end of your relationship. You will be able to see the good that came out of it. No matter how mature you both are... breakups still hurt. You will realize that you can't change someone's mind if they've moved on emotionally. You will see that even if you were somehow able to convince your ex that you shouldn't break up, ultimately that person had already moved on emotionally and spiritually. You'll realize that letting them go will allow you to evolve, grow, and meet other candidates that are better suited to you. Of course, nobody wants to go through a breakup, but sometimes breaking up is better than the alternative...prolonging a relationship where both parties have different goals and objectives.

THE RECOVERY PERIOD

Everyone has experienced a painful breakup and everyone has a different post breakup recovery period. Some may need more alone time; others may need a hot rebound to get back to normal. Everyone's process is different.

After recovering from a breakup, be comforted by the notion that you were able to feel so deeply for someone. Rest assured that if you are open to it, you will feel this deeply again. Allow a breakup to remind you that you were able to get to that place of intimacy with someone. If it can happen once, it can happen again. Don't build an impenetrable emotional wall and carry a past heartache around with you into each new relationship. Allow the possibility of new partners and possibilities to enter into your life.

REBOUNDING

Even though you are on the rebound and looking for fun with someone new, you shouldn't choose just anybody to rebound with. Choose your rebound partners wisely. What starts as a fun, no strings attached sexual escapade could quickly take a turn for the worse if you're not careful. Always be safe, especially when potentially engaging in sex with someone new who you may not know very well. Besides that, you want to cautiously choose someone who knows and agrees with your short-term sexual objectives. *(For more see Ch.8-Sealing The Deal)*

AVOIDING SERIOUS RELATIONSHIPS UNTIL FULLY RECOVERED

Be cautious about getting too serious too soon with someone new after your breakup. If you haven't taken time to heal properly after your breakup and you get serious with someone new, the same issues you dealt with in your last relationship could resurface. You may unconsciously bring past issues into your new relationships or even attract new partners who had similar issues as your ex. Wait until you are in a place where new suitors will have a clean slate with you and don't have to deal with your ex drama. Don't bring old baggage into a new relationship. If you aren't able to go into a new relationship with an open mind, you may not be ready to start dating.

It's unrealistic to expect a new relationship to fix or heal you, not to mention it's unfair to anyone you date. Take as much time as you need to heal before you allow any potential partners to come into the picture. Offer 100 percent of yourself to someone, not a small percentage or the wounded version of your true self. You attract what you are, so get yourself back to 100%, or as close as possible, so you'll more easily attract other singles who are also presenting their best selves.

Present your best self when going through the dating process, not the you that is still in breakup recovery mode. If you are still feeling angry, bitter, or depressed, it may be time to focus more on healing and less on meeting someone new. Consider that whatever energy you bring to a new dating situation, you will get back from your new love-interests. You will attract different people based on the energy you bring to a date. If you're fully recovered and ready to move on from your breakup, you will attract higher caliber dates than if you are still grieving the loss of a past relationship.

A few signs that you're ready to date include….

- *You're having less frequent thoughts about your ex*

- *You're generally happier and have more optimistic feelings attached to dating and meeting someone new*

- *You start noticing attractive people*

- *You meet someone specific that you'd like to get to know better*

Once you've allowed yourself time to heal properly and you're ready to start dating again, do something special for yourself. Get a new haircut. Get a massage. Go on a solo vacation or getaway with friends. Do something for YOU! You've made it through a tough emotional time, so it's also a time to celebrate the new YOU! Reinvent yourself before you re-emerge into the world.

CHAPTER 11

HIBERNATION

Sometimes a dating dry spell can turn into a phase called the 'Hibernation' period. This is a period of several months to a year or possibly longer where you are not actively dating or engaging in sexual activity. It sounds rough, but it can be a beautiful thing. Sometimes after a painful breakup we may slip into this phase. The difference between a slump and Hibernation is that in Hibernation you aren't actively searching for a mate and it is the last thing on your mind. There's no pressure during this phase. You have more time for reflection, self-improvement, hanging out with friends, and simply enjoying your own company and getting to know yourself better. Some of the most productive and creative things can happen during these Hibernation periods.

There are many things you can do when in a dry spell or while 'Hibernating'. Here are things you can participate in at all times regardless of your dating status, but can serve a different purpose when 'Hibernating.'

5 THINGS YOU CAN DO DURING A HIBERNATION PERIOD

1. ATTEND A CULTURAL OR ARTISTIC EVENT FOR INSPIRATION

Find out what's going on in your town. Attend an inexpensive event like an outdoor concert, a book signing, or a poetry reading. Museums sometimes hold special art and music events, especially during the summer months. You are guaranteed to meet interesting people, plus it's a great way to enjoy something artistic and get inspired in the process. These are also places where singles can very easily blend in with the crowd without drawing attention to their solo status.

2. TRY A NEW RESTAURANT

Why not take yourself out to a new restaurant you've always wanted to try? Yes, this can be a bit intimidating, especially on weekends when everyone is out and about. If you feel uncomfortable sitting alone at a table for two, grab a stool at the restaurant's bar. The bartender will check on you periodically and if there are others at the bar, someone is sure to strike up a conversation with you.

3. TAKE A TRIP

Get out of town for a few days! You can take a mini road trip to your neighboring city for a quick change of scenery. Of course ladies should always be vigilant when traveling alone. When it's done right, a solitary adventure can be better than a group or couples getaway!

4. GET A FUN SIDE JOB OR VOLUNTEER

Since you have a little extra time on your hands, why not earn some extra cash or help out in your community? There are tons of side jobs out there from being a dog-walker, to a coffee shop barista. That's a really great way to earn money, meet interesting people, and make new friends in the process.

5. PLAN A RELAXING 'YOU' DAY

These are times when you just want to revel in your own solitude. Take an hour-long bubble bath and just relax or crack open a beer and watch a game. Just do whatever is relaxing to you! It's important to recharge your batteries every so often. By the next day, you'll feel ready to tackle the approaching workweek. It might be unproductive, but it will be totally worth it!

6. RECONNECT WITH FRIENDS AND FAMILY

Our friends and loved ones know us best. These are the people that are there to catch us when we fall, when we fail, and when we're in a Hibernation period or dating dry spell. Spend some quality time with your loved ones. Ground yourself and get reconnected with those closest to you.

7. LEARN SOMETHING NEW

If you don't feel like venturing out, there is plenty to do within your own four walls. You could learn to play an instrument or learn a new language. There are so many fun things you can learn or teach yourself and fortunately you are in a Hibernation period, which means you may have more free time on your hands.

Be careful when coming out of the Hibernation period. After that period has run its course, your sex drive can come back with a vengeance and without warning. This 'coming out of Hibernation' period is similar to the 'rebound phase' after a breakup. You're on the prowl. You're checking everyone out and it sometimes takes effort to keep your hormones in check. These primal feelings can cloud your judgment and cause you to compromise your usual standards. Make a conscious effort to be aware of your feelings, and be as rational as possible. It's great to embrace your reawakening, but also important not to lose yourself in the process.

EPILOGUE

I hope you found something in this book that you can apply to your dating life. You are now ready to fully embrace your single status!

Now that you've learned the basics, the dating process should be less stressful and more enjoyable. Use this book not only to help empower you in your dating life, but also to remind yourself that you hold the key to your own happiness when it comes to being single. Remember when you are too busy looking for "The One," you can very easily miss the joys and perks of being single. Remember to make enjoying yourself and getting to know your date your goal. This will help you make conscious choices and to focus on remaining in the present moment.

Choose to be the single person who can see and appreciate the positive side of dating scenarios yet still be realistic. Make it your goal to make the most out of every date, short-term and long-term partnership. Be excited about the possibilities when you meet someone new. Every date is the beginning of a new adventure. Leave your baggage in the past and start new relationships with a clean slate and an open-mind. Strive to make meaningful connections and relationships a part of your life.

As you enter into different relationships and partnerships, you should be able to look back fondly on all the connections you have made. When you start to enjoy the dating process, your social life becomes a new and exciting adventure. The possibilities are endless. Be open to meeting, greeting, and dating. Consciously choose who you want to date and who you don't want to date. Take your time, be selective but reasonable, remain present, but realistic to more fully enjoy the dating process. You are now on your way to making your single years the best years of your life!

Happy Dating!